Daily Learning Drills

Grade K

Columbus, Ohio

School Specialty Publishing

Copyright © 2004 School Specialty Publishing. Published by Brighter Child®, an imprint of School Specialty Publishing, a member of the School Specialty Family.

Send all inquiries to:
School Specialty Publishing
8720 Orion Place
Columbus, OH 43240-2111

ISBN 0-7696-3090-1

5 6 7 8 9 10 PGL 09 08

Table of Contents

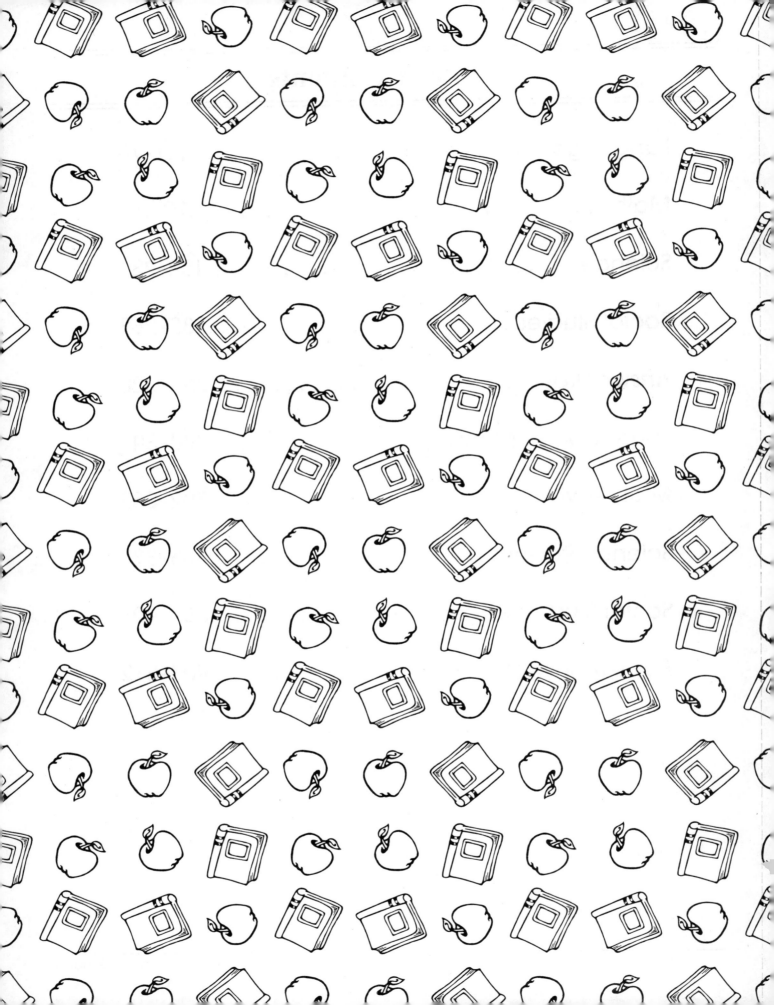

Name _____

Sailing Away

Connect the dots from **A** to **Z**.

Name _____

Let's Play Leapfrog

Help the girl find her way to the frog exhibit. Color the path in order from **N** to **Z**.

Name _____

Sailing Away

Follow the alphabet to lead the pig to the radio.

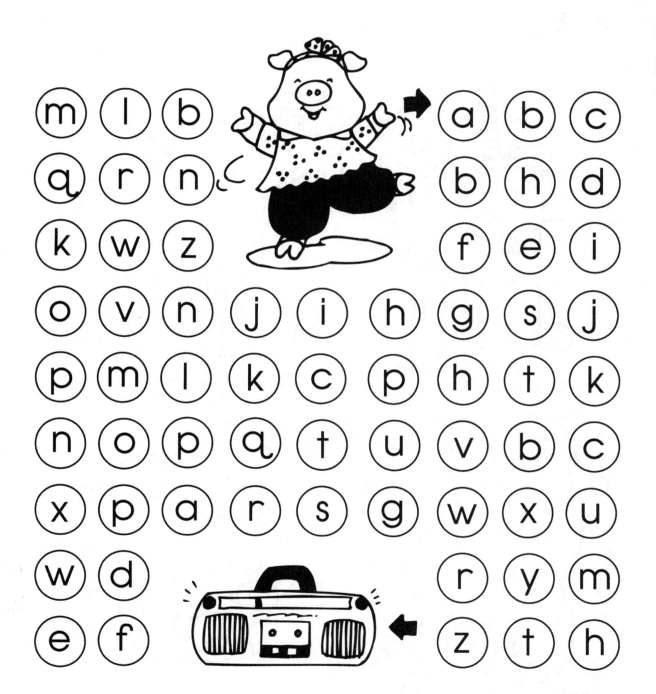

Name _____

Fantastic Farm

Find the letters from **a** to **m**. Color them.

a b c d e f g h i j k l m

Name _____

Trace and Write

Trace the letters. Then write each letter.

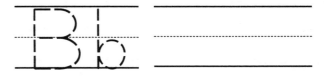

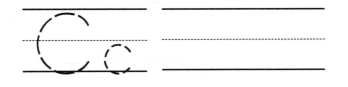

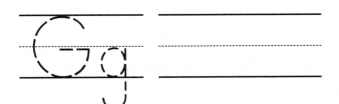

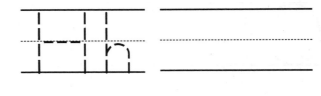

Daily Learning Drills Grade K

Name _____

Trace and Write

Trace the letters. Then write each letter.

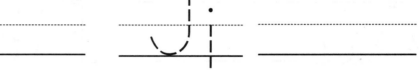

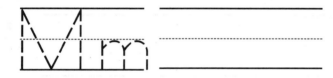

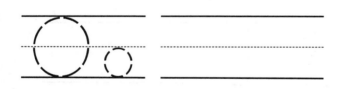
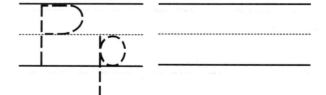

Name _____

Trace and Write

Trace the letters. Then write each letter.

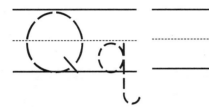

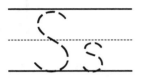

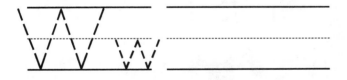

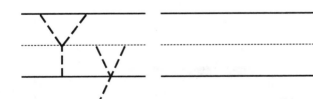
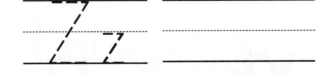

Daily Learning Drills Grade K

Name _____

Letter Trucks

Write the letter that comes between.

Name _____

Letter Matchup

In each row, circle the letters that match the first letter.

B	B	B	R	P
C	Q	O	C	C
D	D	P	D	O
F	P	F	E	F

Name _____

More Matching

In each row, circle the letters that match the first letter.

b	p	b	q	b
c	c	q	o	c
d	p	d	o	d
f	p	f	t	f

Name _____

Letter Garden

Draw lines between the flowers to match the uppercase and lowercase letters.

Aa Bb Cc Dd Ee Ff Gg Hh Ii
Jj Kk Ll Mm Nn Oo Pp Qq Rr
Ss Tt Uu Vv Ww Xx Yy Zz

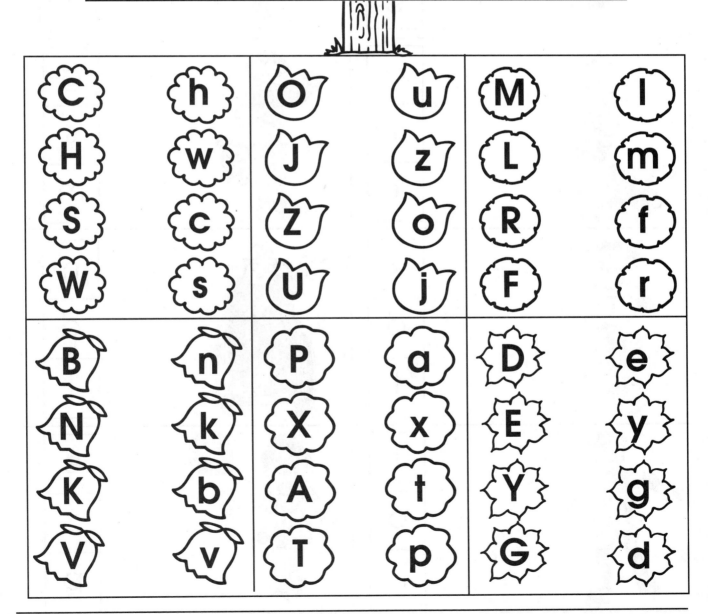

Daily Learning Drills Grade K

Name _____

I Can Match Letters

Draw a line from each child to the matching lowercase letter.

a
m
g

l
w
r

q
l
r

g
s
m

k
o
t

n
d
i

l
o
h

e
z
p

Name _____

Follow the Path

Say the alphabet. Write the missing letters.

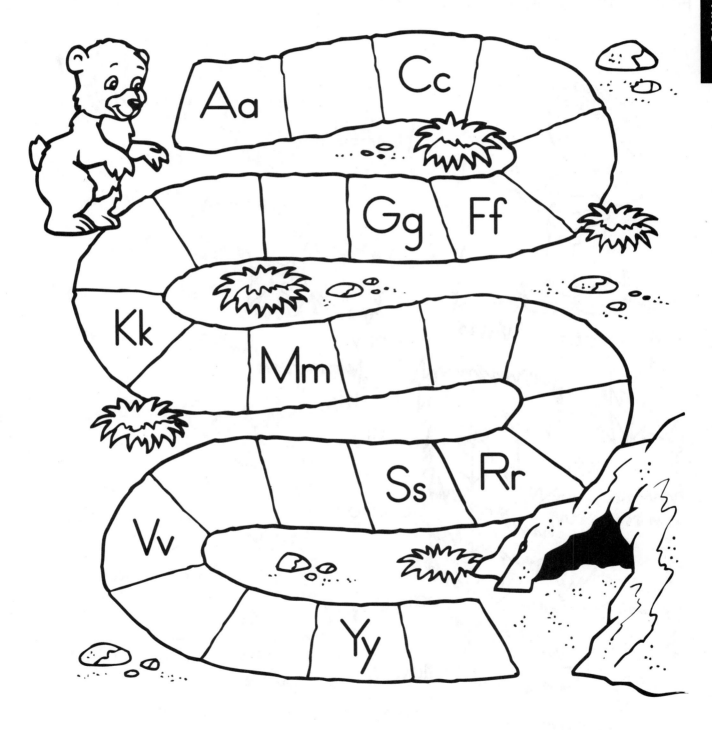

Name _____

A Lost Ball

Help Tommy find his ball.
Follow the words in ABC order.

dog

hair

egg

ape

bunny

cat

gift

cab

donkey

apple

fish

eating

nest

gate

flower

Name _____

Hungry Birds

Help the bird find the worms.
Color the boxes in ABC order.

		ape	hug	fox
		ball	star	gas
deer	cake	cut	door	leg
fan	lake	man	ear	fish
kite	jet	ice	land	goat
lips	king	joke	igloo	hat
map	bed	rose	net	kiss
nose	owl	pet	quit	

Daily Learning Drills Grade K

Name _____

New Word Fun

Write the first letter for each picture.
Write the letters in the boxes to make a new word.

1.

_____ _____ _____

- - - - - - - - - - - - - - - - - - - - - - - - - - -

_____ _____ _____

2.

_____ _____ _____

- - - - - - - - - - - - - - - - - - - - - - - - - - -

_____ _____ _____

3.

_____ _____ _____

- - - - - - - - - - - - - - - - - - - - - - - - - - -

_____ _____ _____

4.

_____ _____ _____

- - - - - - - - - - - - - - - - - - - - - - - - - - -

_____ _____ _____

Fill Them In

Write the vowels to complete each word.

LANGUAGE ARTS

Name _____

The Sound of C

Draw a line from each cat to a picture that begins with the sound of **c**.

Write **Cc**.

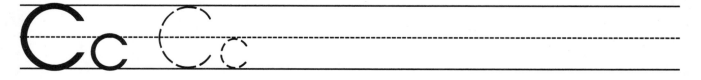

Name _____

The Sound of G

Color the pictures that begin with the sound of **g**.

Write **Gg**.

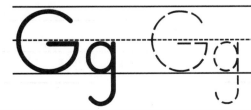

Name _____

The Sound of L

Look at the living room. Draw a circle around five things that begin with the sound of **L**. Color the picture.

Write **Ll**.

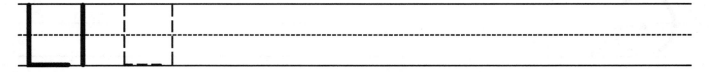

Name _____

Rain, Rain, Go Away

Find these things, which begin with **m**. Color them brown.
Then color the rest of the picture.

mouse   monkey   mop   milk   mask

Name _____

Water Lover

Find these things, which begin with **r**. Color them orange.
Then color the rest of the picture

rose

rake

ring

rocket

raccoon

Name _____

Plump Pig

Color each **u** purple. Then color the rest of the picture.

Name _____

The Sound of Y

Look at each picture. If it begins with **y,** circle **yes.** If it does not, circle **no**.

   yes   no      yes   no

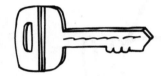   yes   no      yes   no

   yes   no      yes   no

   yes   no      yes   no

Write **Yy**.

Y y

Name _____

All Kinds of Animals

Look at each animal. Say its name. Circle the sound you hear at the beginning of the word.

l   m

r   d

c   f

b   g

j   h

v   w

x   y

q   z

r   s

t   v

h   k

n   p

Name _____

Food Fun

Look at the first picture in each row. Say its name. Then color the picture that has the same beginning sound.

Name _____

Listen Carefully

Look at each column. Color the pictures that begin with the letter shown at the top.

Name _____

Matching Sounds

Draw lines from each letter to the pictures with the same beginning sound.

Name _____

Floating High

Color the words that start with **e** orange.
Color the words that start with **f** yellow.
Write the words under the correct beginning letters below.

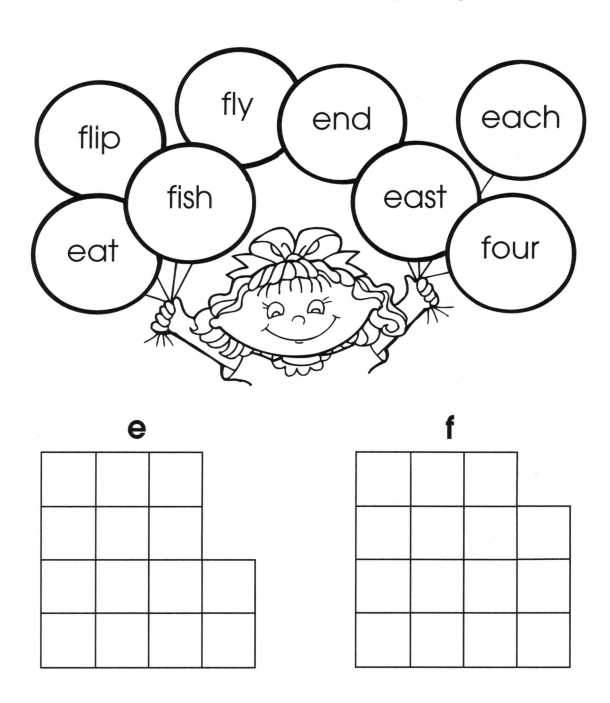

e   **f**

Daily Learning Drills Grade K

Name _____

Scrambled J's, K's, and L's

Unscramble the words that name the pictures.
Write the words.

1.  nkitet _____

2. kngi _____

3. mlap _____

| **Word Box** |
| kite |
| king |
| leg |
| jacks |
| kitten |
| lamp |

4.  elg _____

5.  kiet _____

6. scajk _____

Name _____

Ending Sounds

Listen for the ending sound of each picture. Write it at the end of each word.

ba ____

bu ____

cu ____

he ____

mu ____

Name _____

More Ending Sounds

Listen for the ending sound of each picture. Write it at the end of each word.

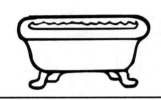

_____

tu

_____

be

_____

fa

_____

ca

_____

to

_____

pi

Name _____

Beginning and End

Say the names of the pictures. Write the letters that make the beginning and ending sounds.

___ a ___

___ o ___

___ a ___

___ o ___

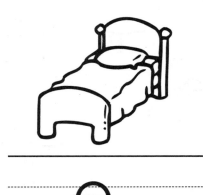

___ e ___

___ u ___

Daily Learning Drills Grade K

Name _____

Discovering Differences

Circle the animal that is different in each column.

Missing Parts

Some of these elephants are missing body parts! Look at elephant **A** to see what's missing on the others. Name the missing body parts and draw them on the animals.

A

B

C

D

Name _____

Parts and Wholes

Complete each picture by drawing the missing piece.

Name _____

What's Different?

Can you find and circle ten ways the bottom picture is different?

Name _____

Opposite Matchup
Draw lines to match the opposites.

Name _____

Ocean Opposites
Draw lines to match the opposites.

little

fast

out

sink

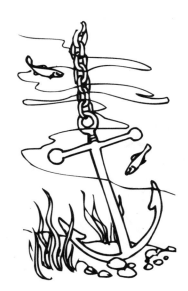

big

in

slow

float

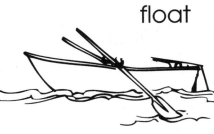

Name _____

Word Match

Match each word with a picture.

cat •

dog •

pan •

ball •

Name _____

Fun Word Match

Match each word with a picture.

plane •

leaf •

bed •

nut •

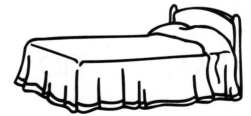

Name _____

Matching Words
Circle matching pairs of words.

go go	sat cat
fox fox	at to
top toe	red red
no no	car cat

Name _____

I Read Words

In each box, circle the words that match the word at the top.

eat
eat   eat
cat   ear

play
play   pay
plan   play

yes
yet   yes
yes   you

take
tack   take
tan   take

me
me   met
men   me

work
walk   work
work   woke

Name _____

Final Question

Match the scrambled letters to find out what the farmer wants to ask.

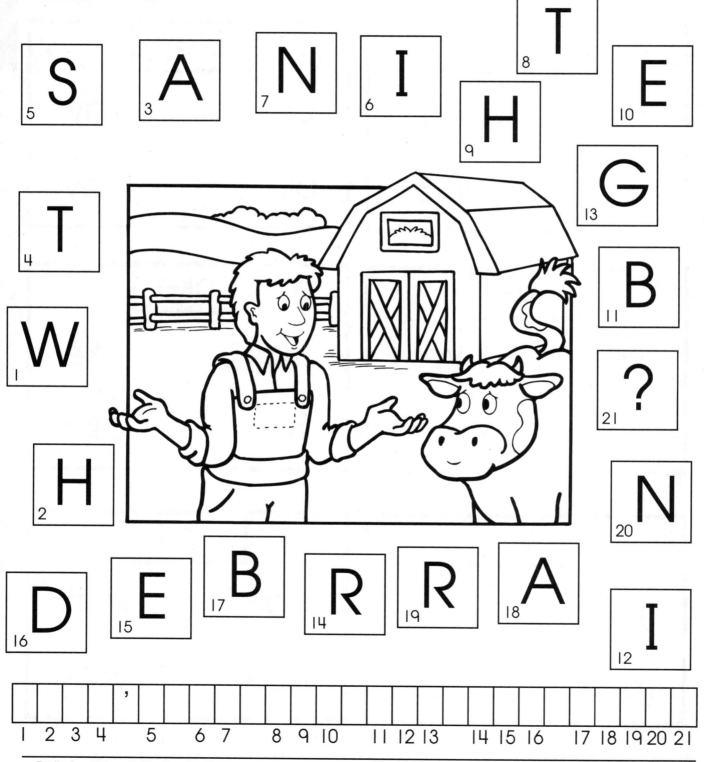

S 5   A 3   N 7   I 6   T 8   E 10

H 9   G 13   B 11

T 4

W 1   ? 21

N 20

H 2

D 16   E 15   B 17   R 14   R 19   A 18   I 12

			'																
1	2	3	4	5	6	7	8	9	10	11	12	13	14	15	16	17	18	19	20	21

Name _____

A Plane

Write the sentence.

See the plane go up.

_____

- - - - - - - - - - - - - - - - - - - -

_____

Find and circle the words. The words go across → and down ↓.

Word Box

up

plane

See

go

the

g	S	e	e	n	p
h	l	s	t	v	l
q	g	z	f	r	a
b	o	m	e	c	n
z	r	k	u	p	e
t	h	e	z	o	w

Name _____

Word Match

Circle the words that match the words at the top of each box.

red sled

red slide

red sled

fun ride

fun ride

fan ride

wet kid

well kid

wet kid

hot fire

hot fire

hot find

Name _____

A Secret Sentence
Color the following words in the puzzle **green**.

| camp | when | test | time |

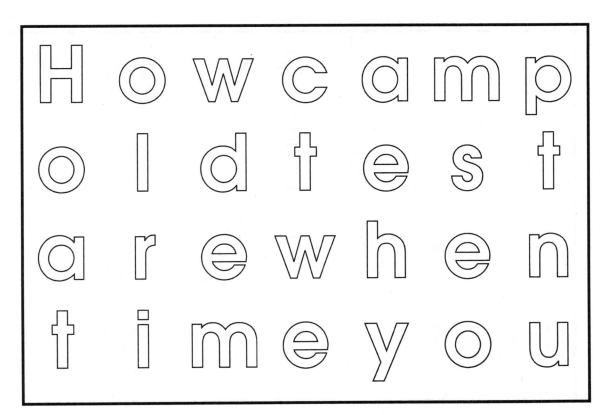

Write the words you did not color to make a sentence.

_____

- -

_____ ?

Name _____

Look and Color
Color the following words red.

| the | was | on | and | but |

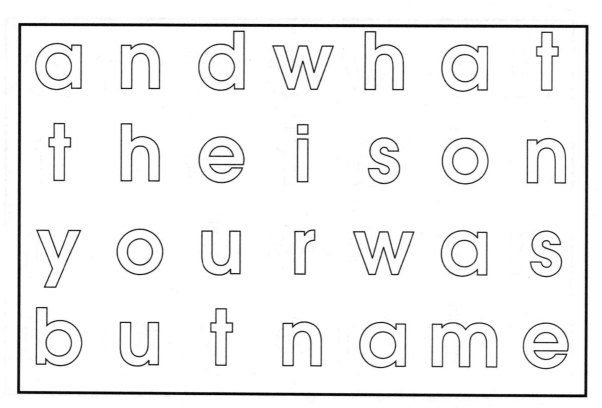

Write the words you did not color to make a sentence.

_____

-- ?

_____

Name _____

New Words

Color the picture. Add the letter. Write the word.

	p	
	.ick	
	l	
	.ick	
	k	
	.ick	
	s	
	.ick	

Daily Learning Drills Grade K

Name _____

Crack the Code

Write the missing letters for each word.
Use the code at the bottom of the page.

1. ⬡ __ __ayon ○ ☆

2. __ou__e ⬠ △

3. __oon ⬠

4. __ta__ △ ☆

5. __lou__ ○ ▢

6. __a__ __ot ○ ☆ ☆

7. bi__ __ ☆ ▢

8. __on__ey ⬠ ◇

c	○
r	☆
s	△
m	⬠
d	▢
k	◇

Name _____

Double Trouble

Write each word in the box next to a word in the puzzle to make a new word.

bell	walk	ground	room
box	ball	fish	print

1. | s | a | n | d | | | |

2. | s | i | d | e | | | |

3. | b | e | d | | | |

4. | s | t | a | r | | | |

5. | f | o | o | t | | | |

6. | b | a | s | e | | | |

7. | d | o | o | r | | | |

8. | c | a | m | p | | | | |

Name _____

Figure Them Out

Unscramble each word. Be sure that it matches the meaning.

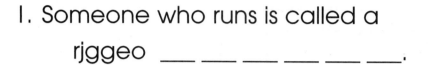

| teacher | ice cream | apple |
| mouse | jogger | tennis |

1. Someone who runs is called a

   rjggeo ___ ___ ___ ___ ___ ___.

2. A game that uses a racket and a small ball is

   stinne ___ ___ ___ ___ ___ ___.

3. Something cold to eat on a hot day is

   cie ramec ___ ___ ___ ___ ___ ___ ___ ___.

4. Someone who teaches children is a

   erhteac ___ ___ ___ ___ ___ ___ ___.

5. A tasty fruit that grows on a tree is called an

   leppa ___ ___ ___ ___ ___.

6. A furry little animal that squeaks is a

   somue ___ ___ ___ ___ ___.

Name _____

At the Bus Stop

Read each question. Answer the question aloud.
Trace the question mark at the end of the question.

Why are the people waiting?

Who has groceries?

Who has a newspaper?

How many kids are waiting?

Name _____

Is It a Question?

Read the sentence. Then repeat it. After repeating the sentence, tell whether it is a question or a statement.

1. My wagon is red.

2. The sky looks cloudy.

3. My favorite colors are red and blue.

4. Do you know where the store is?

5. Is this a difficult activity?

6. I am very tired today.

7. First I wake up and then I brush my teeth.

8. After school I like to play with my friends.

9. What time do you go to school?

10. He helped her ride the bike last Saturday.

Name _____

Words

Write the correct word on each line.

I will go to a _____ .   pond

pool

We need some _____ .   food

rocks

I want to read a _____ .   menu

book

I can help the _____ .   cat

dog

Name ____________________

Color Craze

Follow the directions for each coloring activity.

1. Color the items you can eat.

2. Color the objects you write with.

3. Color the toys.

4. Color the fruit.

5. Color the capital letters.

B d y F i M

Name _____

I Can Have Fun
Color the things that go together in each row.

LANGUAGE ARTS

Name _____

In the Middle
Color each object that is in the middle.

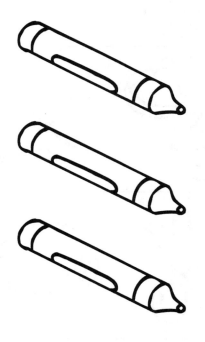 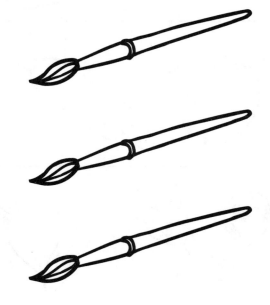

Name _____

Top, Middle, Bottom

Look at the picture. Who is at the **top** of the hill? Who is at the **middle** of the hill? Who is at the **bottom** of the hill? Fill in the blanks below.

The dog is at the _____ of the hill.

The cat is at the _____ of the hill.

The boy is at the _____ of the hill.

Name _____

In or Out

Look at each picture. Circle whether the clown is **in** or **out**.

in   out   in   out   in   out

in   out   in   out   in   out

Name _____

Color Words
Say the color names. Color the pictures.

red

orange

yellow

green

blue

purple

black

brown

Daily Learning Drills Grade K

Name _____

What a Great day!

Read the color words. Color the spaces to match.

Name _____

More Color Words

Trace the words. Say the color names.
Color the crayons.

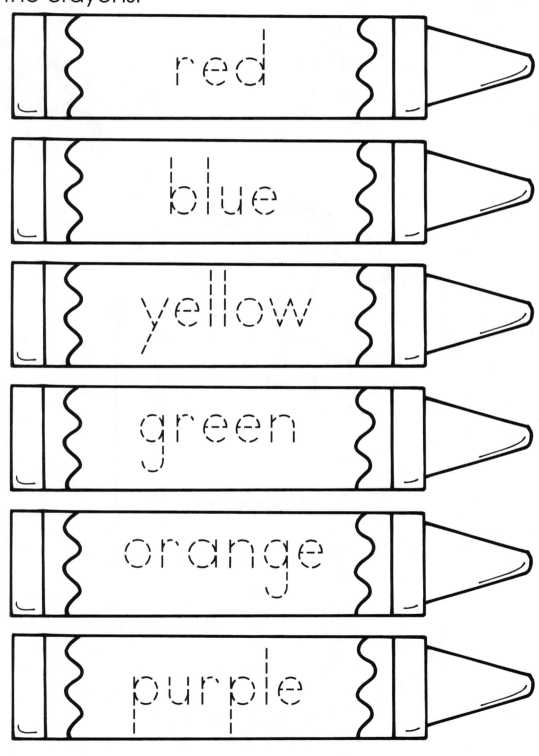

Name _____

A Tisket, a Tasket

Follow the directions to color the basket.

1. Color one flower red.
2. Color one flower blue.
3. Draw a bow on the basket.
4. Color the basket green and yellow.
5. Draw another flower in the basket.

Name _____

Make a Picture

Follow the directions to complete the picture.

1. Draw a tree to the right of the school.

2. Draw a sun in the top left of the picture.

3. Draw a flag to the left of the school.

4. Draw some flowers to the right of the tree.

5. Draw a picture of yourself to the left of the school.

Name _____

I Enjoy Books

Circle and write the best title for the picture.

Eating Dinner

Books for Sale

We Like to Read

_____

- -

_____

- -

_____

Name _____

Can It Really Happen?

Does each picture show something
that can really happen?
Circle **yes** if it does.
Circle **no** if it does not.

yes

no

yes

no

yes

no

yes

no

yes

no

yes

no

Name _____

Funny Garden

Does each picture show something that can really happen?
Circle **yes** if it does.
Circle **no** if it does not.

yes

no

yes

no

yes

no

yes

no

yes

no

yes

no

Name _____

LANGUAGE ARTS

Rhyme Time

Color. Draw lines to match the rhyming words.

ring

bug

bell

tree

rug

shell

king

bee

Name _____

Time to Rhyme

Use the picture clues to match the rhyming words.

1. meat

2. seal

3. king

4. mouse

5. clock

6. hair

7. dog

8. boat

 sock

 wheel

 bear

 ring

 goat

 frog

 feet

 house

Name _____

Before and After

Look at the picture in the middle. Draw something that happens before and after. Trace the words.

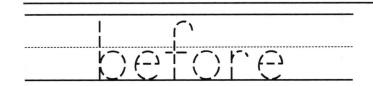

Name _____

Draw a Dinosaur

These pictures are out of order. Number the steps from 1 to 6.

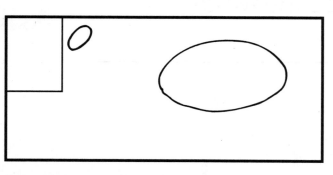

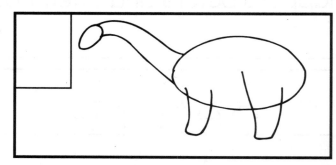

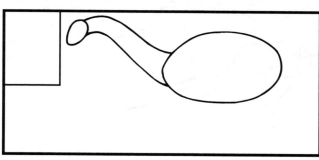

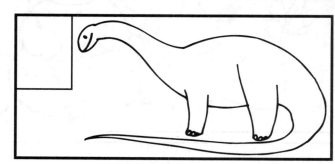

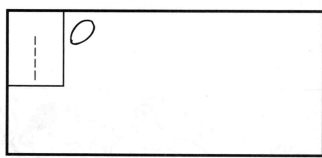

Follow the steps to draw a dinosaur.

Name _____

My Day at Kindergarten

Read the story below. Then cut out and place the sentences in sequential order.

When the bell rings it is time to go inside. First, the teacher reads a story. Then we have a snack. Finally, we do an art project. At 12:00, it is time to go home.

	When the bell rings it is time to go inside.
	Then we have a snack.
	Finally, we do an art project.
	At 12:00 it is time to go home.
	First, the teacher reads a story.

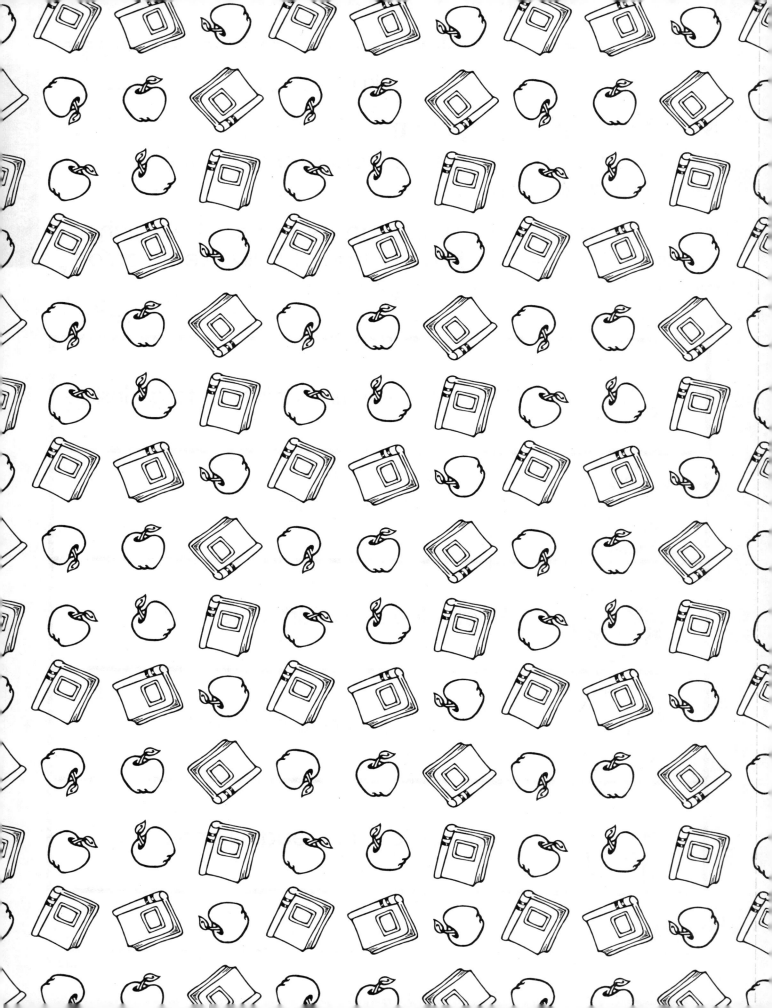

Name _____

Sailing Fun

Read a story about Matt and his dad.

Matt and his dad enjoy sailing. When they sail, they like to listen to music. Matt likes fast, loud music. His dad likes slow, soft music. Matt and his dad have lunch on the boat, too. Matt likes hot dogs. His dad likes ham sandwiches.

Put an **X** in the box or boxes that answer each question.

Matt and his dad are alike. They both like

☐ sailing

☐ music

☐ hot dogs

Matt and his dad are different.

For lunch, Matt likes a

☐ ham sandwich    ☐ hot dog

For lunch, his dad likes a

☐ ham sandwich    ☐ hot dog

Name _____

What Happens Next

Draw a line to match the cause to the effect.

Cause   **Effect**

Name _____

I Can Circle What Happens Next

Circle the picture that shows what will happen next.

Daniel threw a stick across the yard for his dog, Muffy.

Muffy will take a nap.

Muffy will run to get the stick.

Rachel wrote a letter. She put it in an envelope and put a stamp on it.

Rachel will put the letter in the mailbox.

Rachel will put the letter in the bathtub.

The cake was cool. Tyler got the bowl of frosting.

Tyler will cut the cake.

Tyler will frost the cake.

Name _____

One, Two, Buckle My Shoe

Say the nursery rhyme. Clap out the beat.
Make one clap on each **bold** word.

One, two,
Buckle my **shoe**.

Three, **four**,
Shut the **door**.

Five, **six**,
Pick up **sticks**.

Seven, **eight**,
Lay them **straight**.

Nine, ten,
A **big** fat **hen**.

Size Search

Cut out the animal cards below. Glue each animal under the correct size.

small	medium	big

Name _____

The Pick of the Garden

Circle the animal that is biggest in each row.

Robin   **Grasshopper**   **Beetle**

Butterfly   **Rabbit**   **Snail**

Caterpillar   **Hummingbird**   **Squirrel**

Name _____

Perfectly Pleasing Patterns

Circle the object that comes next.
Color the pictures.

Name _____

Grow a Garden

Circle the item that comes next in each row.

Name _____

Animal Parade

Circle the animal that comes next in each parade.

   |

 |

 |

   |

Daily Learning Drills Grade K

Name _____

Drawing Shapes

Trace.   Draw.

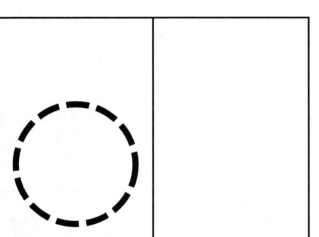

Circles

Trace.   Draw.

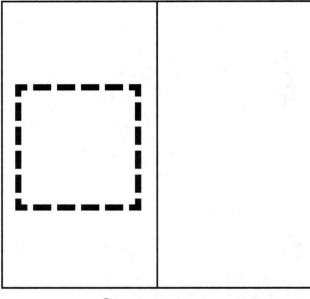

Squares

Trace.   Draw.

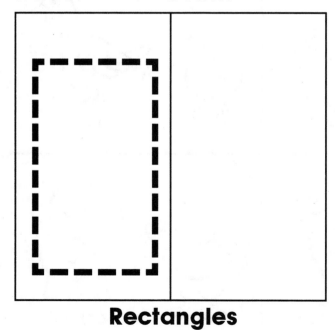

Rectangles

Trace.   Draw.

Triangles

Name _____

Floating Up

Color **6**  orange.

Color **7** blue.

MATH

Name _____

Shape Words

Trace and say the shape word. Draw lines to match the shape word to the object.

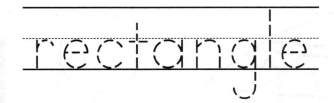

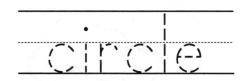

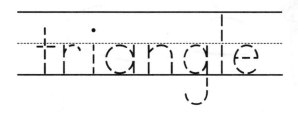

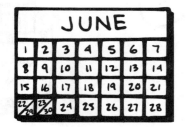

Name _____

Other Shapes

Trace and draw.

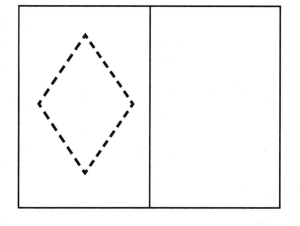
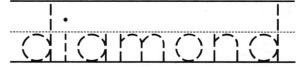

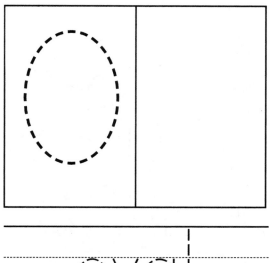

oval

heart

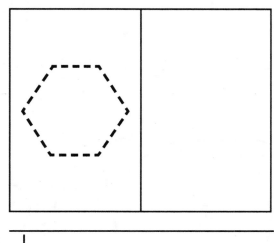
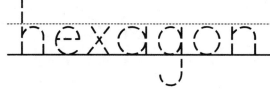

hexagon

Name _____

Fun on the Farm

Find the circles, triangles, and squares.
Color them. Color the rest of the picture.

Name _____

Matching Shapes

Look at each row. Say the shape name.
Color the objects that have the same shape.

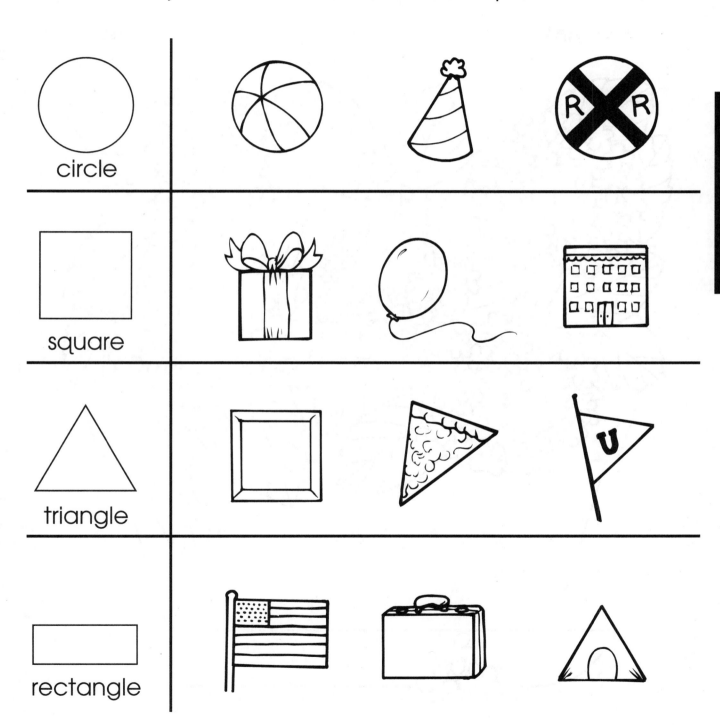

Name _____

A Blooming Success!

Color the flower blossoms.
Use the number key to help you.

1 = pink   **2 = blue**   **3 = purple**

Name _____

A Yummy Number

To find the mystery number, color the spaces with these numbers purple.

9   5   8   7   10   13   18   17   20   19

Circle the mystery number.   **5   10   18**

Name _____

Water Wonder

Color to find the hidden picture.

5 = yellow   **7** = green   **10** = blue

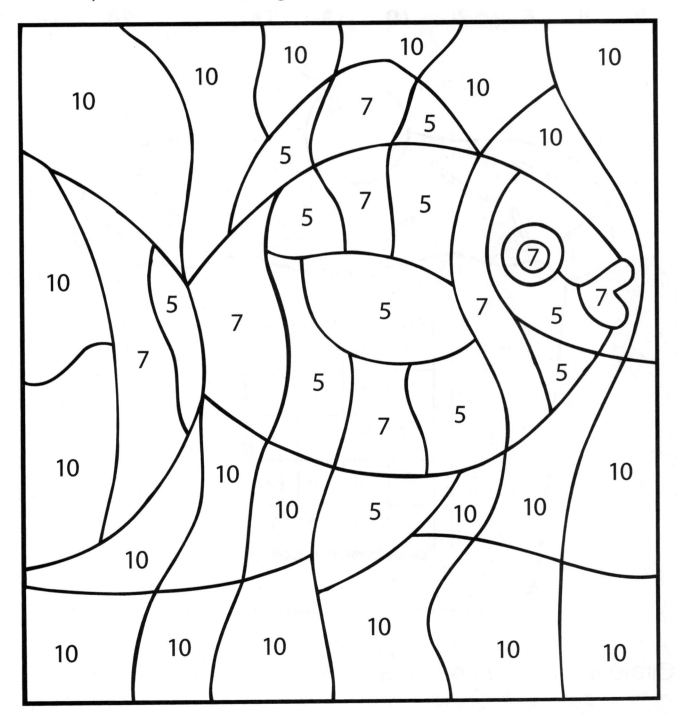

Name _____

Polly Want a Cracker?

Color to find the hidden picture.

13 = green   **14** = orange   **15** = yellow

Daily Learning Drills Grade K

MATH

Name _____

Floating Away

Color to find the hidden picture.

18 = blue   **19** = red   **20** = yellow

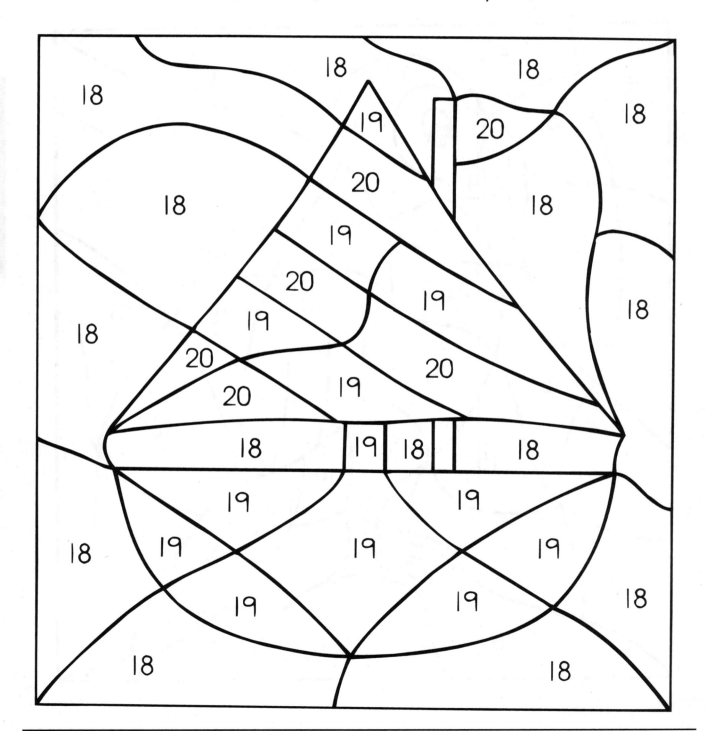

Name _____

Count and Write

Trace the numbers.

1	2	3	4	5
6	7	8	9	10

Write the numbers from 1 to 10.

1	2	__	4	__
__	7	__	9	__

__	2	3	__	__
6	__	8	__	10

Daily Learning Drills Grade K

Name _____

Let's Count

Write the missing numbers.

Name _____

Number Connector

Connect the number words in order.
Then color the number you made.

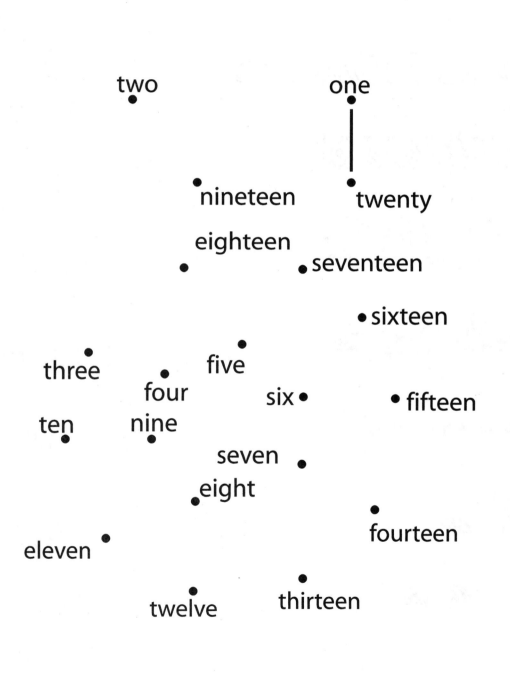

1	one
2	two
3	three
4	four
5	five
6	six
7	seven
8	eight
9	nine
10	ten
11	eleven
12	twelve
13	thirteen
14	fourteen
15	fifteen
16	sixteen
17	seventeen
18	eighteen
19	nineteen
20	twenty

MATH

Name _____

Count and Match

Count. Draw a line to the correct number word. Trace each number word.

seven

three

five

nine

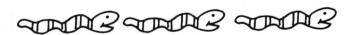

four

six

eight

Name _____

Counting Critters

Count the things in each group. Write the number word in the boxes by the pictures.

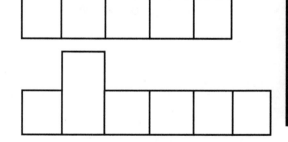

1 one	2 two	3 three	4 four
5 five	6 six	7 seven	8 eight
9 nine	10 ten	11 eleven	12 twelve

1.

2.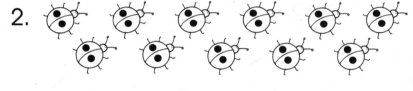

3.

4.

5.

6.

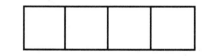
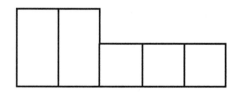
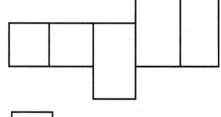
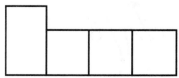

Daily Learning Drills Grade K

Name _____

Not a Dragon

Connect the dots from **1** to **12**. Color to finish the picture.

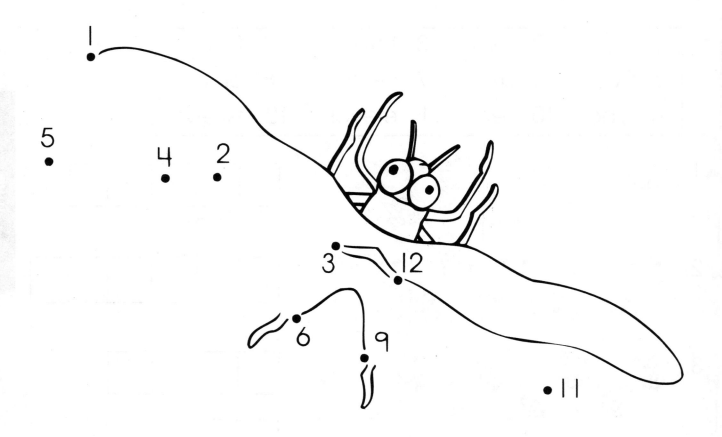

Name _____

Balancing Trick

Connect the dots from **1** to **20**. Color to finish the picture.

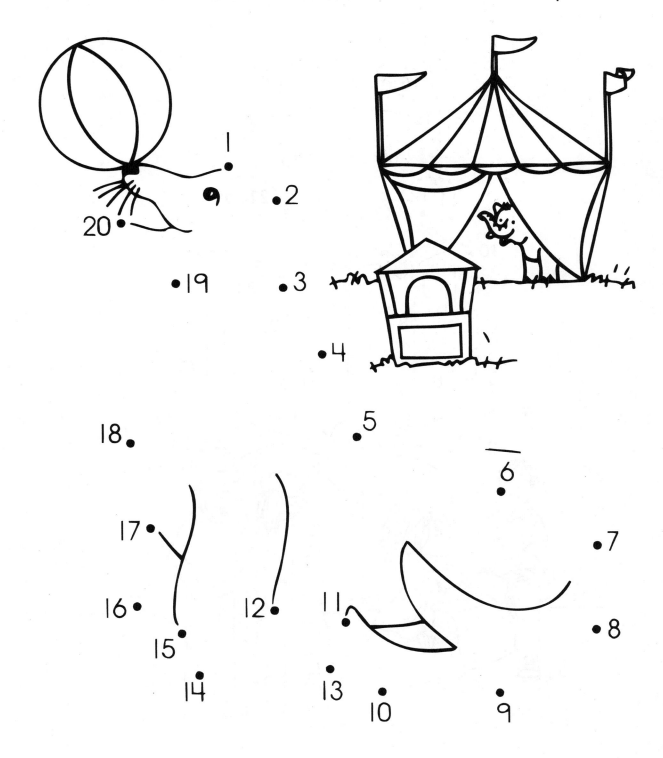

Daily Learning Drills Grade K

Name _____

In the Town Square

Connect the dots to see what is in the town square.

Name _____

Making Music

Color the sets of 3.

3

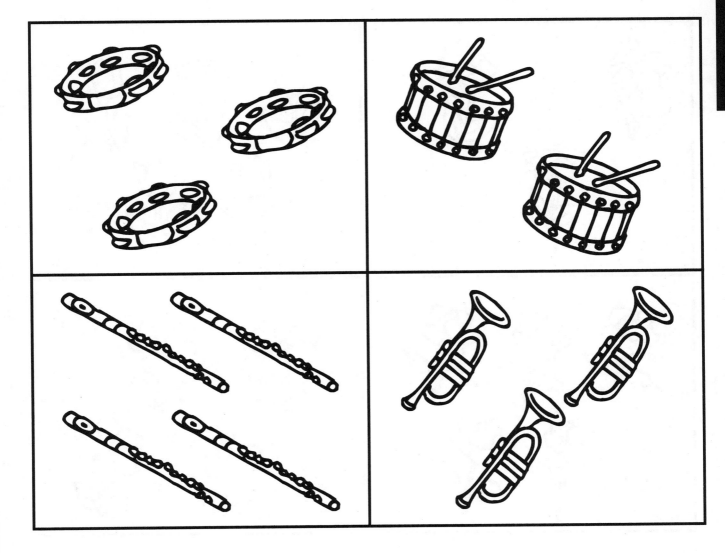

Daily Learning Drills Grade K

Name _____

Flower Power

Color the sets of 5.

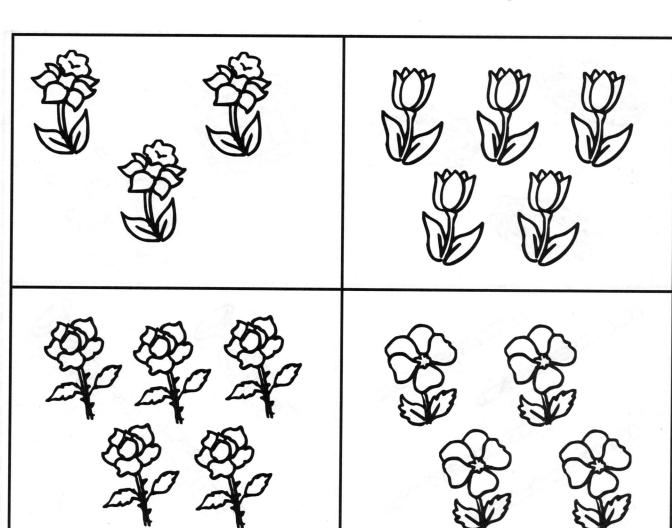

Name _____

Mouse Lunch

Find the food and color it green. Then color the rest of the picture.

Circle to show how many.

 1 2 3   1 2   1 2 3   1 2 3

Daily Learning Drills Grade K

Name _____

Farm Count

Count the objects. Write the number.

Name _____

Gardening Counting

Count the objects. Write the number.
Circle the smaller number.

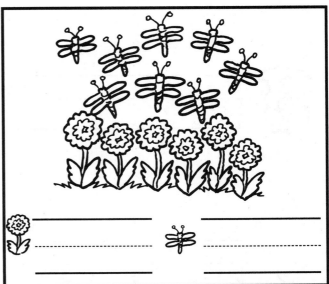

Daily Learning Drills Grade K

Name _____

Barnyard Hoedown

Count the animals and trace the letters below. Color.

  seven   eight

 nine   ten

Name _____

Bird Buddies

Find the numbers **1** to **10** in the picture. Color them.

Daily Learning Drills Grade K

Name _____

I Can Count

Count and color.

Color 1.

Color 2.

Color 3.

Color 4.

Color 5.

Name _____

It's a Ten

Draw more objects to make ten in each set. Then color the pictures.

1.

2.

3.

4.

5.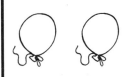

MATH

Name _____

Tally It Up

Use tally marks to show how many objects are in each box.

I	I I	I I I	I I I I	⦀⦀	⦀⦀ I
1	2	3	4	5	6

Name _____

Count the Objects

Count. Circle the number.

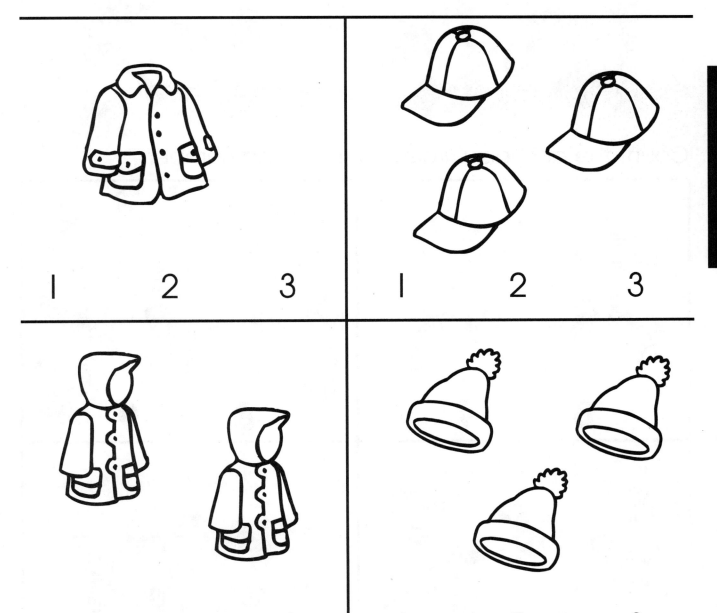

1   2   3

1   2   3

1   2   3

1   2   3

Name _____

Animals in Winter

Count the animals. Circle the matching number.

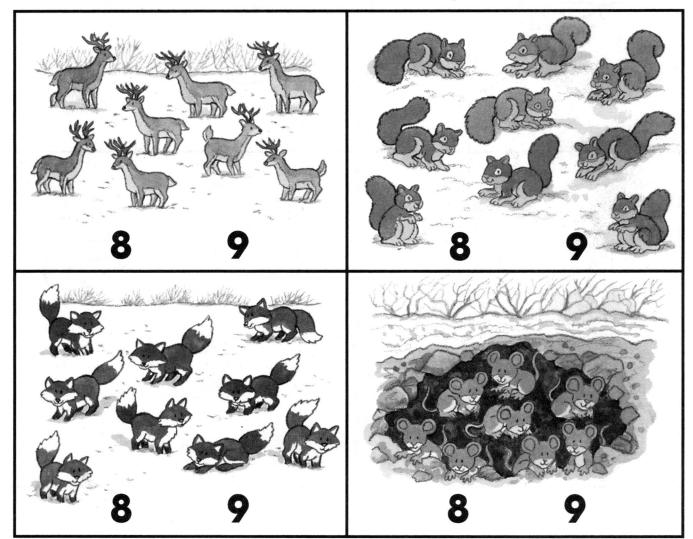

Name _____

Super Circles

Count the circles. Color them.

Circle to show how many circles you found.

11   **12**   **13**   **14**   **15**   **16**   **17**   **18**   **19**   **20**

Name _____

Spotty Leopards

Circle the number of spots on each leopard.

Name _____

I Can Write Numbers

Trace. Count and circle the pictures.

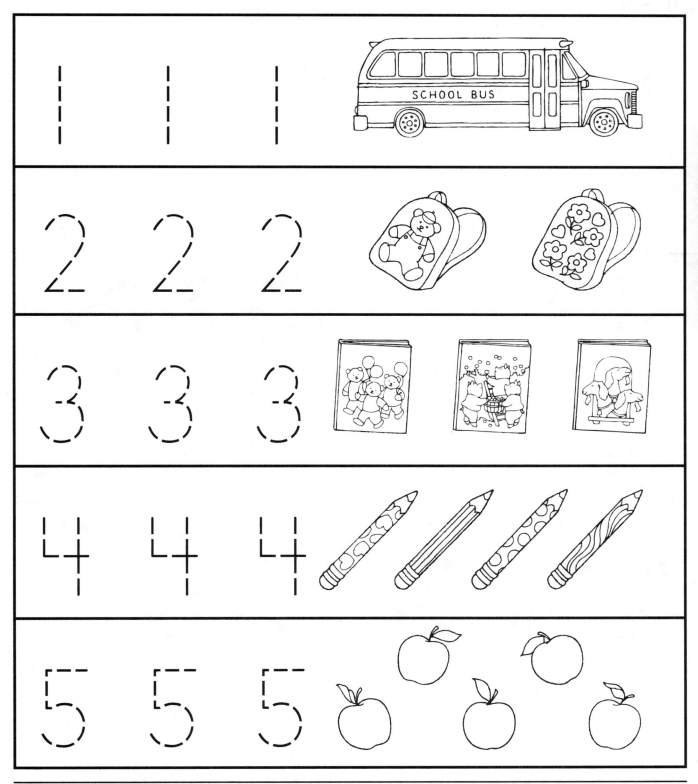

Name _____

Clean and Healthy

Trace the number that tells how many.

0   1   2

0   1   2

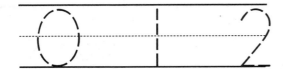

2   3   4

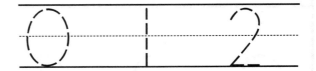

5   6   7

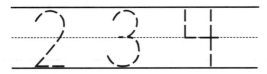

5   6   7

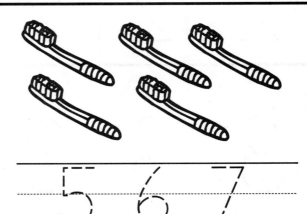
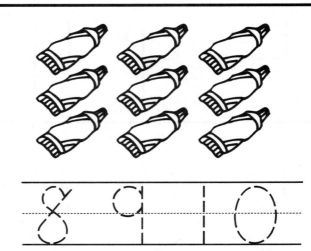

8   9   10

Name _____

Elephant Snacks

Count the peanuts in each bag.
Then write the number on the line.

Daily Learning Drills Grade K

Name _____

Stringing Numbers

On each string, draw enough beads to show
the number.

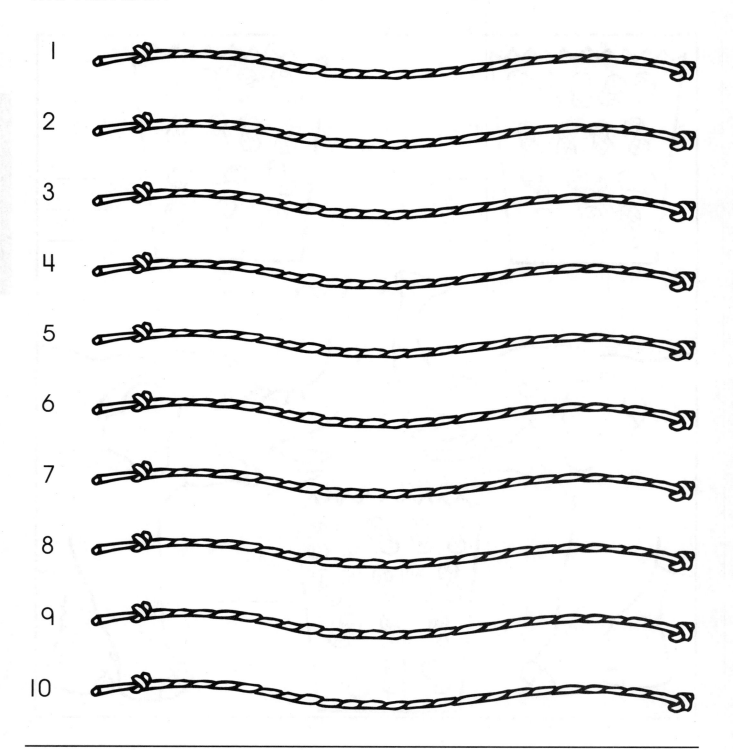

1

2

3

4

5

6

7

8

9

10

Name _____

Mouse Hunt

Find **10** mice below. Color them.
Color the rest of the picture.

Daily Learning Drills Grade K

Name _____

Nut Hunt

Find the nuts . Color them brown. Then color the rest of the picture. Can you find **I I** nuts in all?

Name _____

Big Jumpers!

Find the grasshoppers . Color them green.
Then color the rest of the picture. Can you find **12**
grasshoppers in all?

Daily Learning Drills Grade K

Name _____

Monkeying Around

Find the bananas . Color them yellow. Then color
the rest of the picture. Can you find **15** bananas in all?

Name _____

Color Creations

Find the crayons . Color them purple. Then color the rest of the picture. Can you find **18** crayons in all?

Daily Learning Drills Grade K

Name _____

Feeding the Birds

Draw **15** more pieces of birdseed in the bag.
Then answer the question below.

How many pieces of birdseed are in the bag now? _____

Name _____

Clever Clover

Look carefully at the picture. Find the **25** hidden shamrocks. Color them green.

MATH

Name _____

Fish Bowl

Color **20** fish.

Circle to show how many fish are left over.　　**5**　　**6**　　**7**

Name _____

Snail Garden

Color **25** snails brown  .

Circle to show how many snails are left over.   **3**   **4**   **5**

MATH

Name _____

Piggy Bank

Color **24** pennies brown  .

Circle to show how many pennies are left over. **2   3   4**

Name _____

Which Is More?

Count the objects in each group. For each row, circle the group with the larger number. Then color the objects.

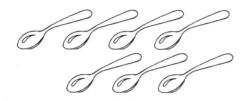 OR

 OR

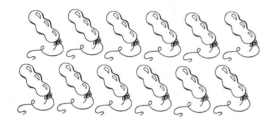 OR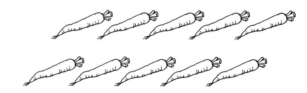

 OR

 OR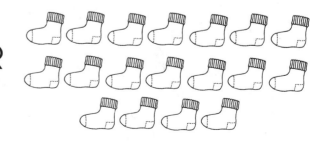

Daily Learning Drills Grade K

MATH

Name _____

Finding Friends

Help Tommy Turtle find his friends.
Color the path that goes in order
from **1** to **8**.

Name _____

I Can Play

Draw a path to each toy by counting from 1 to 9.

MATH

Daily Learning Drills Grade K

Name _____

Ready to Land

Count from **1** to **20** to take the plane to the hangar.

4	2	1

6	3	8	7	8	9	10	7	12

5	4	5	6	3	15	11	8	13
9	2	11	13	14	13	12	1	2
10	14	17	16	15	9	13	4
3	16	5	17	18	19
15	11	8	9	13	20

Name _____

A–mazing–ing Football

Get Freddy Football to the end zone by counting by 2s. Starting with 2, color the footballs that contain numbers counting by 2 until you reach the end zone and score a touchdown.

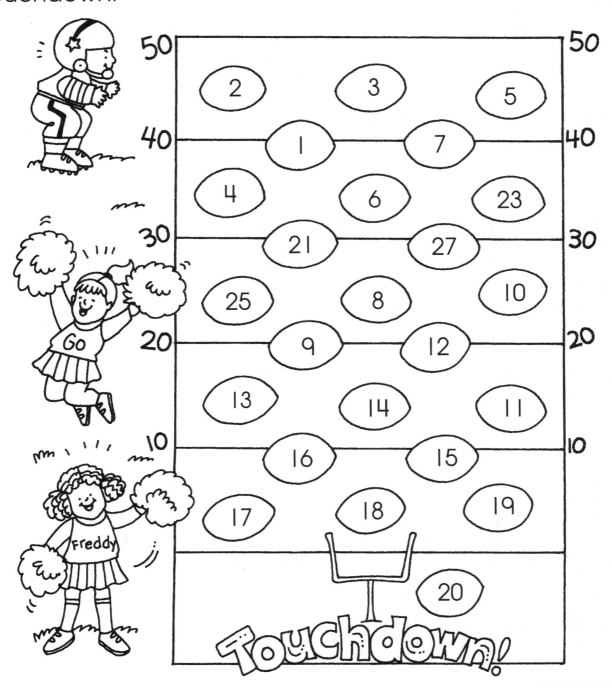

Name _____

Crazy Counting

Trace. Write the missing numbers.

Count by twos.

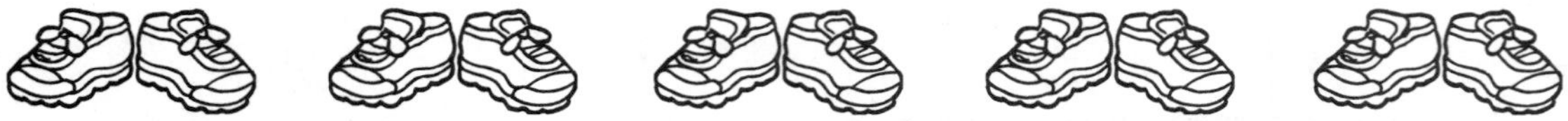

2 ___ 6 8 ___

Count by fives.

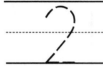  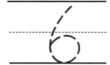 

5 10 ___ 20 ___

Count by tens.

10 ___ 30 ___ 50

Name _____

Add them Up

Write the numbers that tell how many.

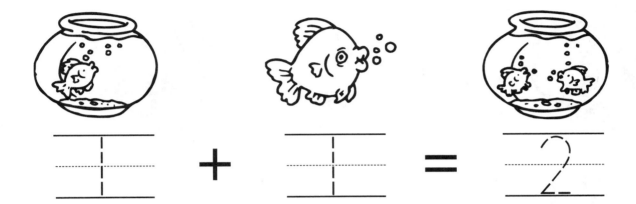

$$\underline{\quad 1 \quad} \; + \; \underline{\quad 1 \quad} \; = \; \underline{\quad 2 \quad}$$

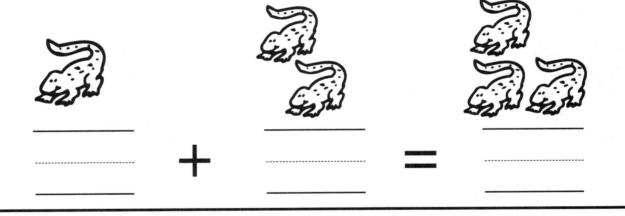

$$\underline{\qquad} \; + \; \underline{\qquad} \; = \; \underline{\qquad}$$

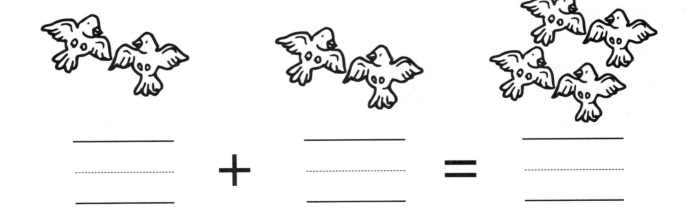

$$\underline{\qquad} \; + \; \underline{\qquad} \; = \; \underline{\qquad}$$

MATH

Name _____

How Many in All?

Write the numbers that tell how many.

___2___   +   ___2___   =   ___4___

_____   +   _____   =   _____

_____   +   _____   =   _____

Name _____

A Special Friend

Add. Then color to find a special friend.

3 = green   **4 = blue**   **5 = brown**

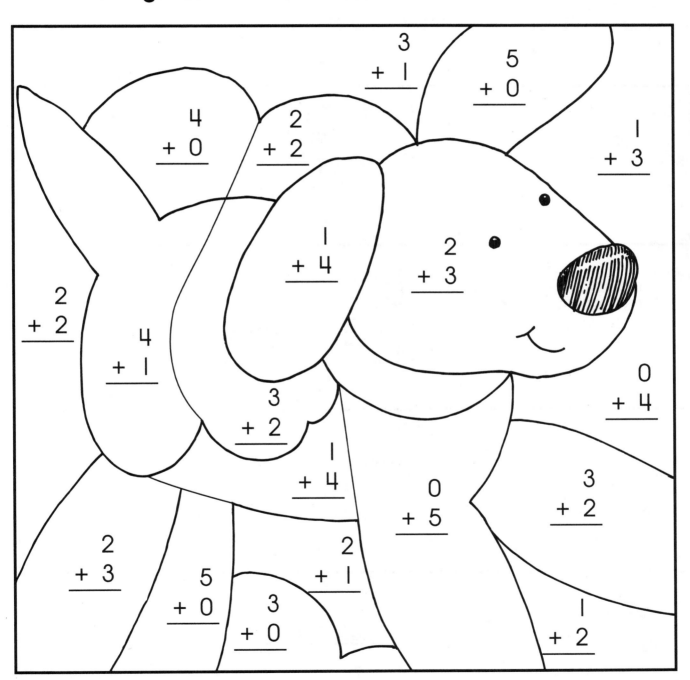

Name _____

Add 'Em Up

Add the numbers.

 2 +  3 = _____

 1 +  6 = _____

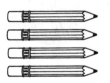 4 + 4 = _____

 2 +  4 = _____

 5 + 2 = _____

Name _____

Starry Sums

Add the stars in each row. Write the sum on the line.

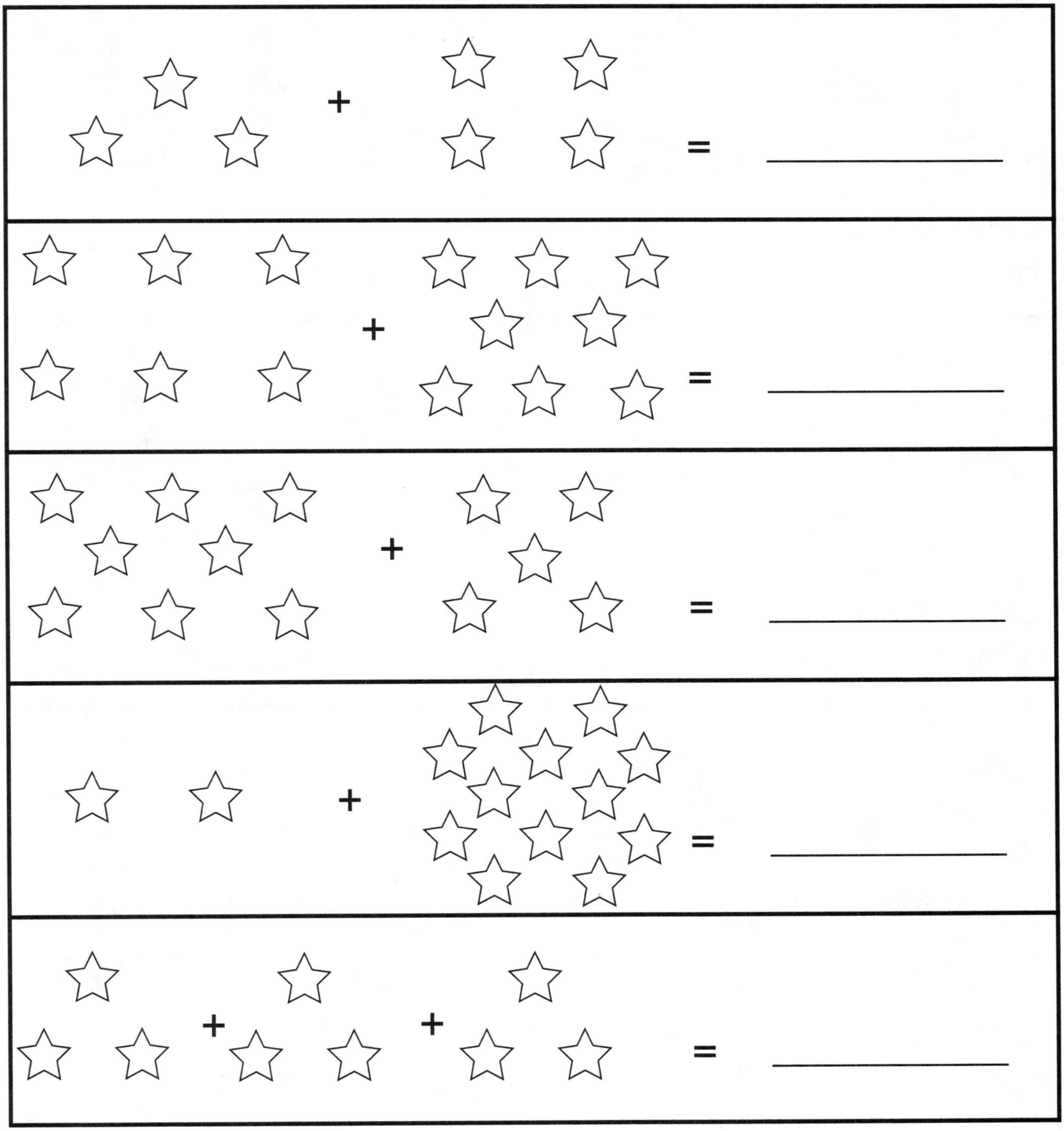

☆☆☆ + ☆☆ ☆☆ = _____

☆☆☆ ☆☆☆ + ☆☆ ☆☆☆ ☆☆☆ = _____

☆☆☆ ☆☆ + ☆☆ ☆ ☆☆☆ ☆☆ = _____

☆ ☆ + ☆☆ ☆☆☆☆ ☆☆☆☆ ☆☆ ☆☆ = _____

☆ ☆ ☆ + + ☆☆☆☆ ☆☆ = _____

MATH

Name _____

In the Garden

Cross out 1.
How many are left? _____

Cross out 3.
How many are left? _____

Cross out 1.
How many are left? _____

Cross out 2.
How many are left? _____

Cross out 2.
How many are left? _____

Cross out 2.
How many are left? _____

Name _____

Where Did They Go?

Any animal that has been crossed out is gone.
How many animals are left? Circle the number.

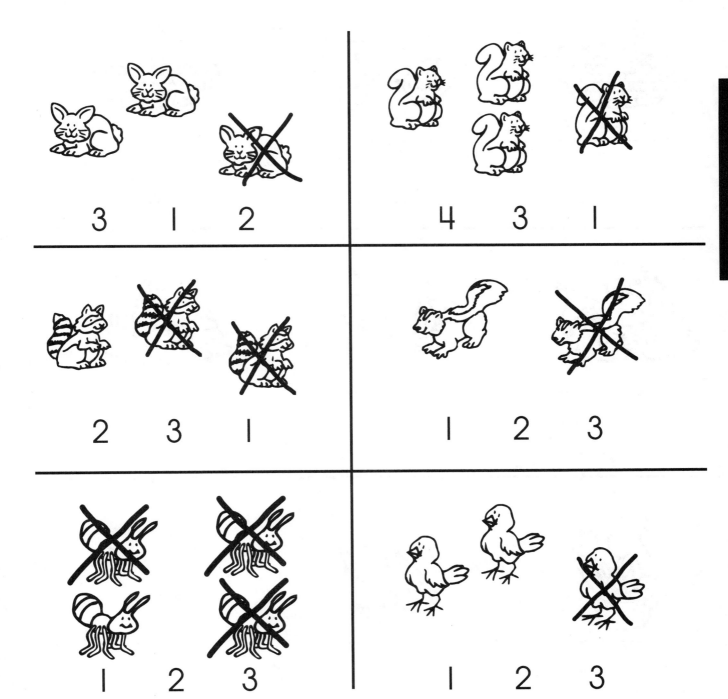

3   1   2

4   3   1

2   3   1

1   2   3

1   2   3

1   2   3

MATH

Name _____

How Many Are Left?

Write the numbers that tell how many.

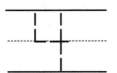 — 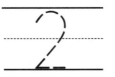 =

$$4 - 2 = 2$$

 —  = _____

_____ — _____ = _____

_____ — _____ = _____

Name _____

Wholes and Halves

Look at the vegetables at the bottom of the page. Draw two halves next to the matching whole vegetable.

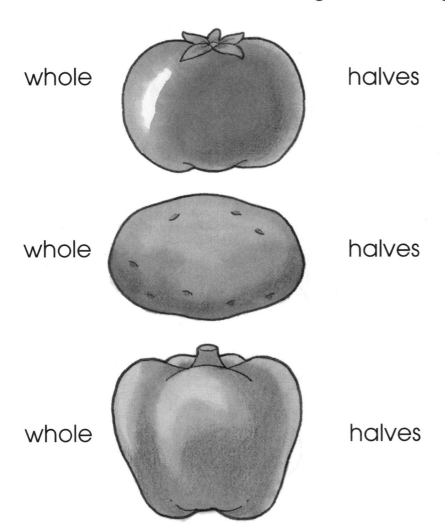

whole   halves

whole   halves

whole   halves

Daily Learning Drills Grade K

Name _____

Half and Half

Look at the pictures below. Make each object whole by drawing its other half.

1.

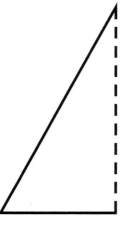

2.

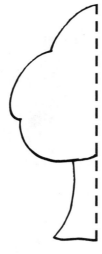

3.

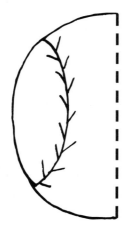

4.

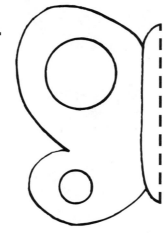

5.

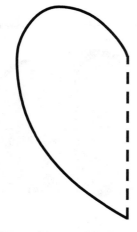

6.

Name _____

Where's the Turtle?

Write the place of the turtle.

first   **second**   **third**   **fourth**   **fifth**

first   second   _____   fourth   fifth

first   second   third   fourth   _____

first   _____   third   fourth   fifth

Name _____

Friends Go Hiking

The friends are following their leader on the trail.
Draw a line from each number-order word to the matching hiker.

fourth   third   first   second   eighth   fifth   seventh

Name _____

Money Mania

Add the coin values in each row. Write the total amount on the line.

penny 1¢	nickel 5¢	dime 10¢	quarter 25¢

1. = _____

2. = _____

3. = _____

4. = _____

5. = _____

6. = _____

7. = _____

8. = _____

9. = _____

10. = _____

MATH

Name _____

Money Matters

Add the coin values in each row. Write the total amount on the line.

penny 1¢	nickel 5¢	dime 10¢	quarter 25¢

1.		= _____
2.		= _____
3.		= _____
4.		= _____
5.		= _____
6.		= _____
7.	 	= _____
8.	 	= _____
9.	 	= _____
10.	 	= _____

Name _____

What's Long?

Color the two in each set that are the same length.

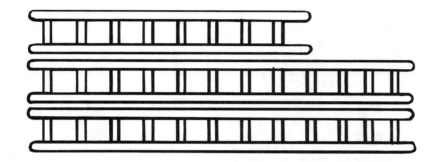

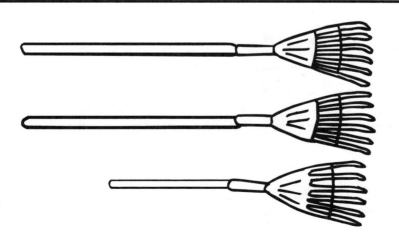

Daily Learning Drills Grade K

Name _____

Dinosaurs Rule!

Scientists use rulers to measure dinosaur bones.
Write the missing numbers on the rulers.

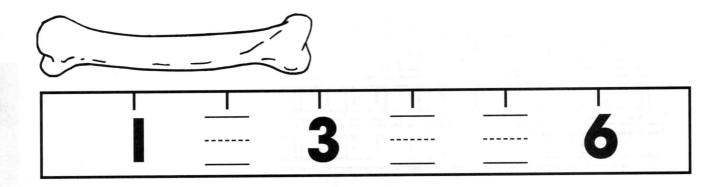

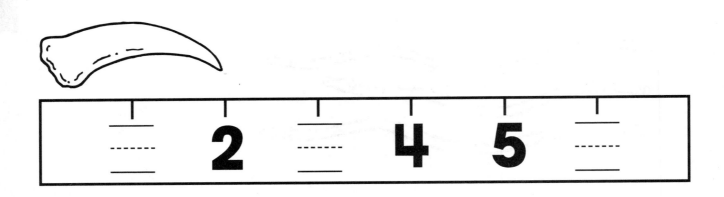

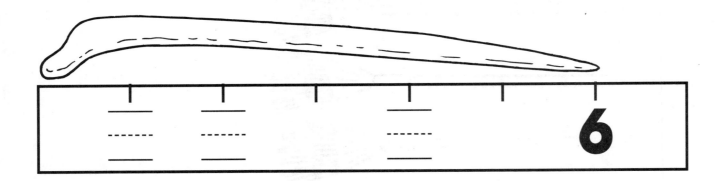

Name _____

I Can Measure

Draw a line from each child to the correct measuring tool.

Name _____

Animal Graphs

Write how many. Circle the animal that has the most. Color the animal that has the least.

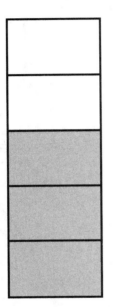

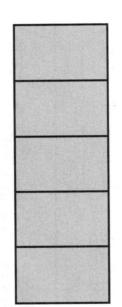

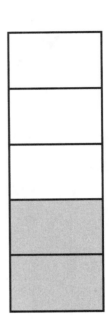

_____

_____

_____

Name _____

Funny Frogs

Count the frogs and write the number.
Color a square for each frog.

2 ___   ___   ___   ___

4				
3				
2				
1				

Name _____

Days of the Week

Trace the words. Say them.

The first day of the week.

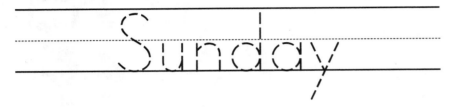

The second day of the week.

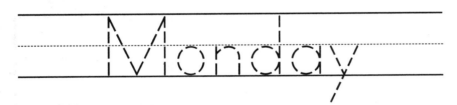

The third day of the week.

The fourth day of the week.

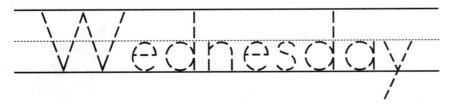

Name _____

More Days of the Week

Trace the words. Say them.

The fifth day of the week.

The sixth day of the week.

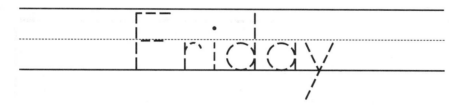

The seventh day of the week.

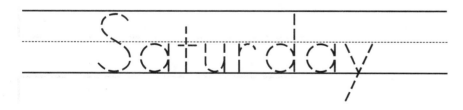

What's your favorite day of the week?

_____

- - - - - - - - - - - - - - - -

_____

Name _____

Time of Day

Trace and color. Draw a picture of something you do during each time of the day.

Name _____

Body Parts

Point to the body parts. Say the name of each.
Trace the words.

head

arm

hand

leg

foot

Name _____

Left and Right

Draw a ring on the right hand.
Draw a watch on the left wrist.

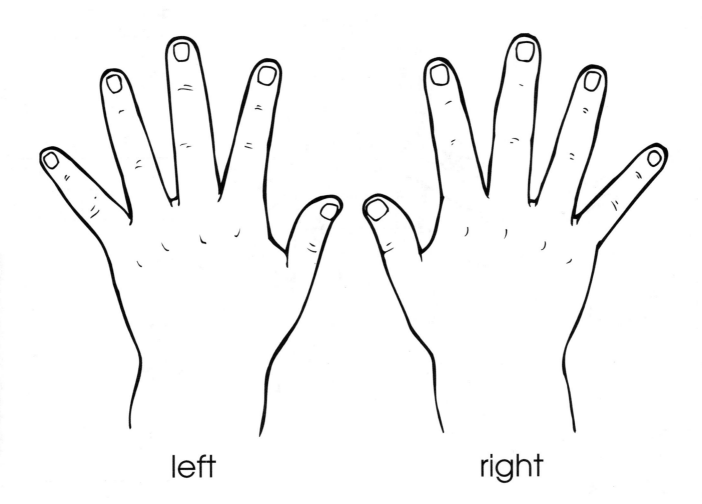

left   right

When you draw or write, which hand do you use?

_____

_____

Name _____

My Hair

Draw a picture of your face and hair.

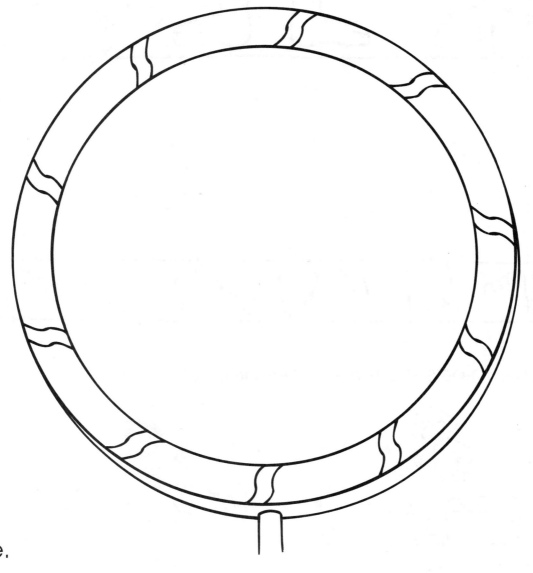

Circle.

My hair is _____.
straight   curly   wavy

The color is _____.
brown   black   red   blond

Name _____

My Feet

Draw a picture of your feet.

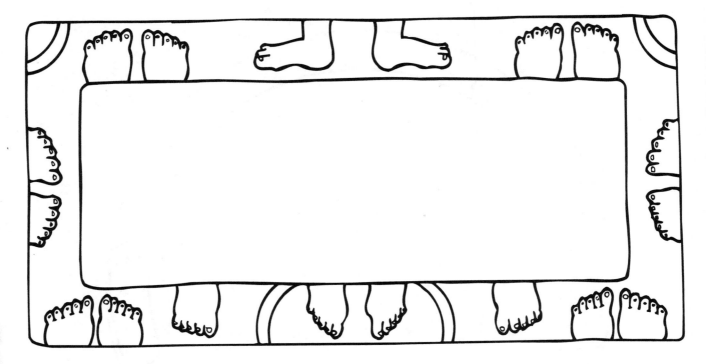

Color the things that your feet help you do.

Name _____

My Five Senses

Which parts of the body help you see, hear, smell, taste, and touch? Draw lines to show your answers.

I see with my

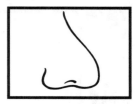

I hear with my

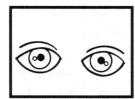

I smell with my

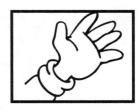

I taste with my

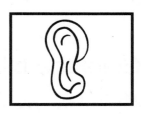

I touch with my

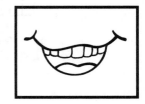

Name _____

My Eyes

Draw a picture of your eyes.

Color the things you like to see.

Name _____

My Ears

Draw a picture of your ears.

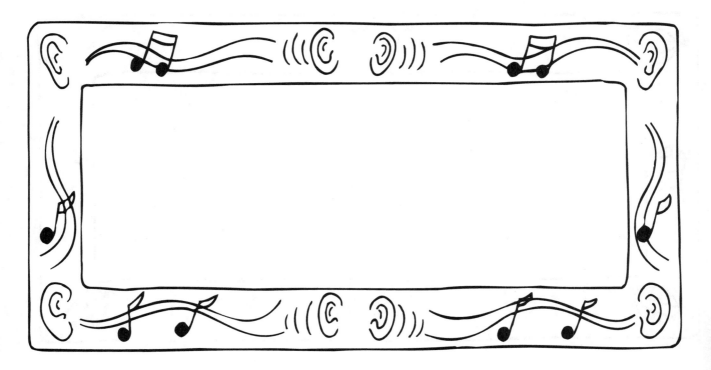

Color the things you like to hear.

SCIENCE

Name _____

My Mouth

Draw a picture of your mouth and teeth.

Color the things you like to eat.

Name _____

My Hands

Draw a picture of your hands.

Color the things you like to touch.

Daily Learning Drills Grade K

SCIENCE

Name _____

I Brush My Teeth

Circle the things that you use to brush your teeth.

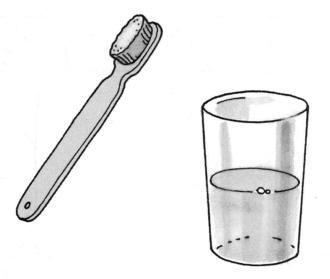

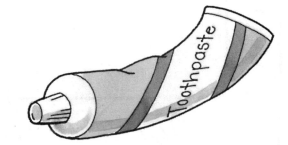

Draw a picture of yourself
brushing your teeth.

Brush your teeth,
Clean and floss,
Show those cavities
Who's the boss!

Name _____

I Am Growing

_____

I weigh _____ pounds.

_____

I am _____ inches tall.

Color the things that help you grow.

SCIENCE

Name _____

I Eat Healthful Snacks

Circle six healthful snacks.

Name _____

Healthy Hang-Ups

Create a mobile using the pieces below. Color these foods and cut out. Punch holes at the top of each piece and hang from a clothes hanger or dowel.

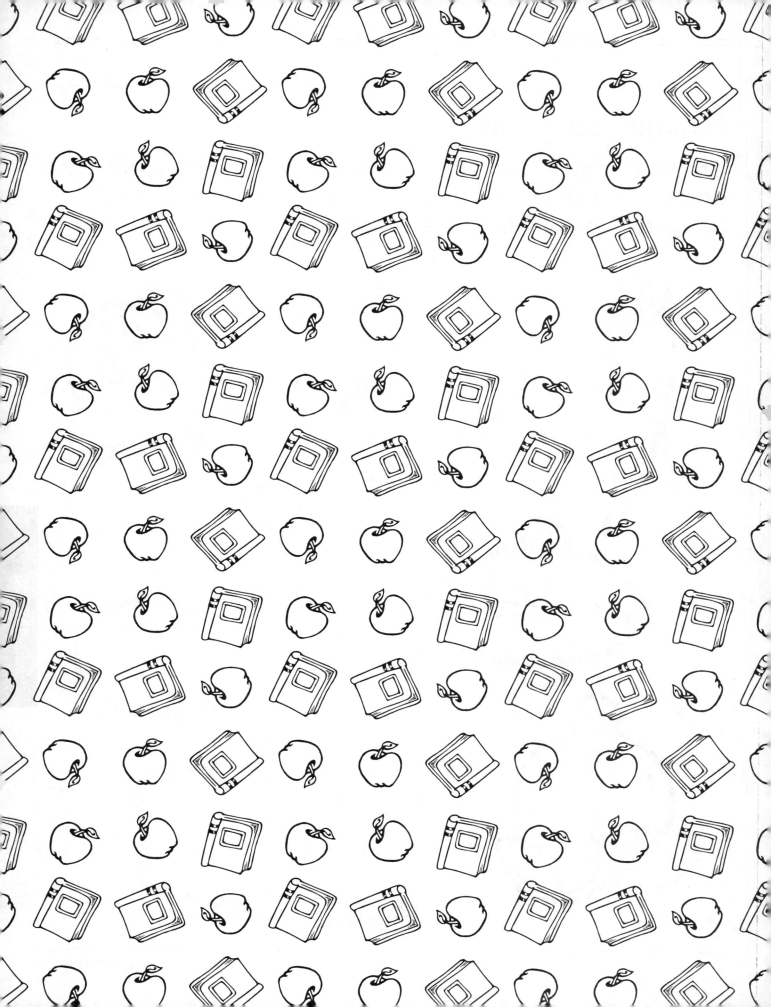

Name _____

Let's Eat Dinner!

Read each sentence. Draw a line to the matching picture.

I will eat spaghetti.

I will eat green beans.

I will eat bread.

I will eat a cupcake.

SCIENCE

Name _____

My Favorite Food

Finish the sentence. Draw a picture to match.

My favorite dinner meal

is

My favorite drink is

Here is what I like to eat for dinner.

Name _____

Plant at Work

Cut out the pictures. Match and paste them in order.

The seed is planted in soil.

A root grows down into the soil.

The stem pushes up toward the sun.

The stem grows and leaves unfold.

SCIENCE

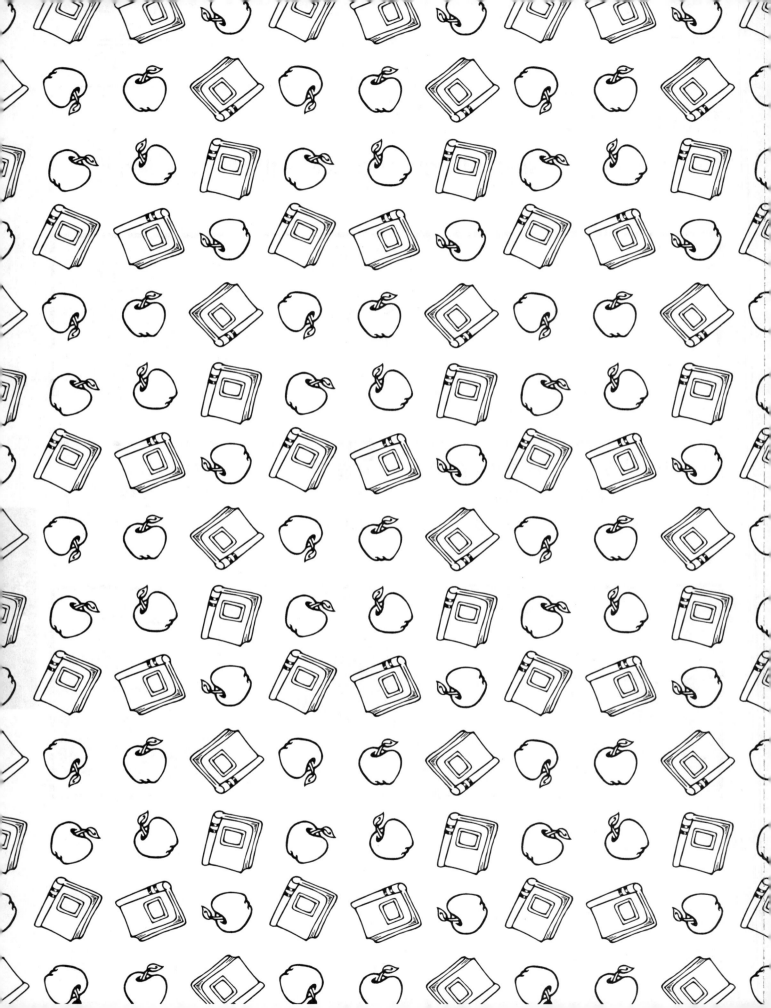

Name _____

Plant Fun

Find the word in each row. Color the boxes to show the word.

seed

root

stem

dirt

sun

water

leaf

s	e	e	d	x
b	r	o	o	t
s	t	e	m	p
d	i	r	t	l
a	s	u	n	k
w	a	t	e	r
t	l	e	a	f

SCIENCE

Name _____

Parts of a Plant

Trace the words and the lines. Color the plant.

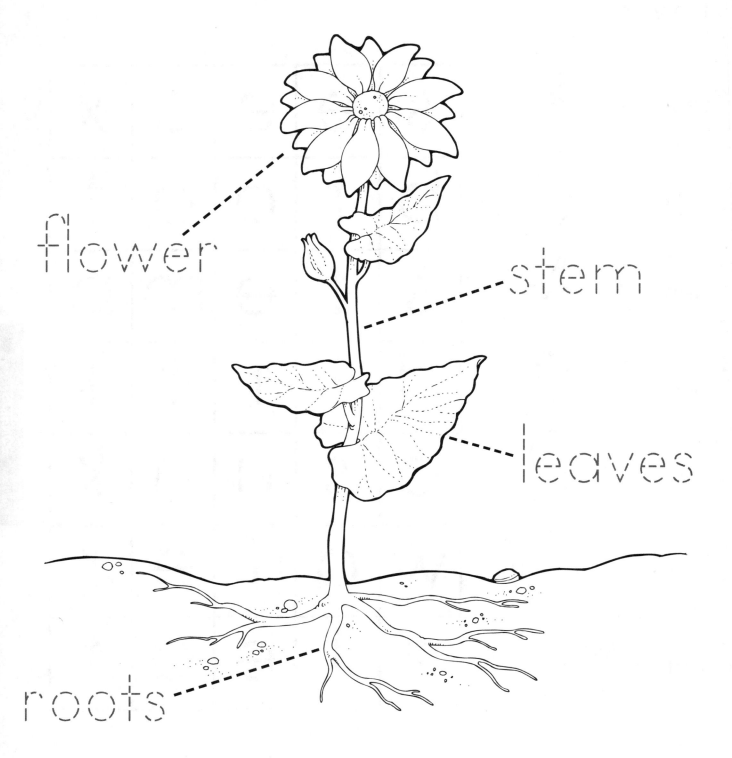

Name _____

Eating Plants

Trace the words.

We Eat Parts of

corn

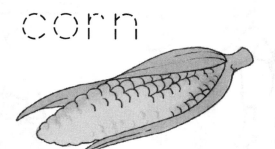

We eat seeds.

carrots

We eat roots.

celery

We eat stems.

lettuce

We eat leaves.

apples

We eat fruits.

Name _____

At the Market

Look at the picture. Find **3** foods. Write their names.

1. _____

2. _____

3. _____

Name _____

Plants We Eat

Circle the words. The words go → and ↓.

k	p	u	m	p	k	i	n	l
c	i	f	n	u	c	l	a	e
e	f	s	c	a	r	r	o	t
l	y	b	r	g	d	q	d	t
e	m	p	c	o	r	n	w	u
r	o	v	z	m	v	j	h	c
y	e	b	e	a	n	s	r	e

 carrot

 corn

 lettuce

 pumpkin

 celery

 beans

SCIENCE

Daily Learning Drills Grade K

Name _____

Plant Groups

Cross out the plant in each box that does not belong.
Color the other plants.

Name _____

Trees Give Many Gifts

Circle the pictures that show ways people use trees and things that come from trees.

SCIENCE

Name _____

A Special Garden

Draw a picture of yourself standing in a garden.

Describe what you see standing in the garden.

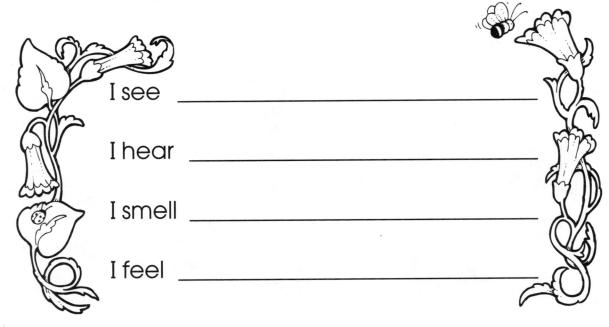

I see _____

I hear _____

I smell _____

I feel _____

Name _____

Garden Days

Circle and write the best title for each picture.

A Long Nap

No More Weeds

Smell the Flowers

_____
- -
_____

A Sweet Lunch

A Big Bird

Trees Are Green

_____
- -
_____

SCIENCE

Name _____

Out of Place

Circle **1** thing in each box that does not belong.
Answer the question at the bottom.

Everything circled is a kind of what?_____

Name _____

In the Forest

Look at the picture. Find **3** living things.
Write their names.

_____

1. _____

2. _____

3. _____

SCIENCE

Name _____

At the Farm

Look at the picture. Find **3** living things.
Write their names.

1. _____

2. _____

3. _____

Name _____

Pets We Like

Color the pictures. Say the words. Check off the pets you have or would like to have.

☐ turtle

☐ bird

☐ snake

☐ dog

☐ cat

☐ rabbit

Name _____

How Animals Move

Tell how each animal moves. Trace the words.

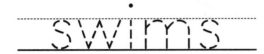

swims

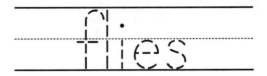

flies

jumps

climbs

runs

hops

Name _____

Flying High

Color the things that fly.

SCIENCE

Name _____

I Want My Mommy!

Trace the line from each baby to its mother.

Name _____

Little Lost Lamb

Help the lamb find its mother.

SCIENCE

Name _____

Mrs. Cow's Friends

Trace the names of Mrs. Cow's barnyard friends. Color.

1. horse

2. piglets

3. rooster

4. lamb

5. dog

6. mouse

7. cat

Name _____

Search and Find

Find the objects in the woods. Color them.

deer   eggs   squirrel   fish   frog   snake

SCIENCE

Daily Learning Drills Grade K

Name _____

A Beaver Family

Help the beavers get out of their house.

Name _____

The Zoo

Finish each sentence with the name of an animal.

bear   **monkey**   **snake**   **zebra**

I see a _____ .

I see a _____ .

I see a _____ .

I see a _____ .

Name _____

Hear Me Roar!

Connect the dots from 1 to 10. Color.

Name _____

Where Are the Tigers?

Help the boy find his way to the tigers.

SCIENCE

Name _____

Zoo Puppets

You can create paper bag puppets to look like your favorite zoo animals. Just follow these simple directions.

Get a paper bag that fits easily over your hand. You will make your head on the end of your paper bag. The side with the fold will be the front of your animal's head. Draw or paste on your animal's eyes and nose. Don't forget to add ears on the back of the head.

Put your hand inside the paper bag and move the fold up and down with your hand. This part of the bag will be the mouth. Draw or paste on teeth and a tongue.

Decorate the front of the bag to look like the body of your animal. Add a tail if you need to!

Name _____

Train Safari

Help the train take the right path through the forest.
Watch out for elephants!

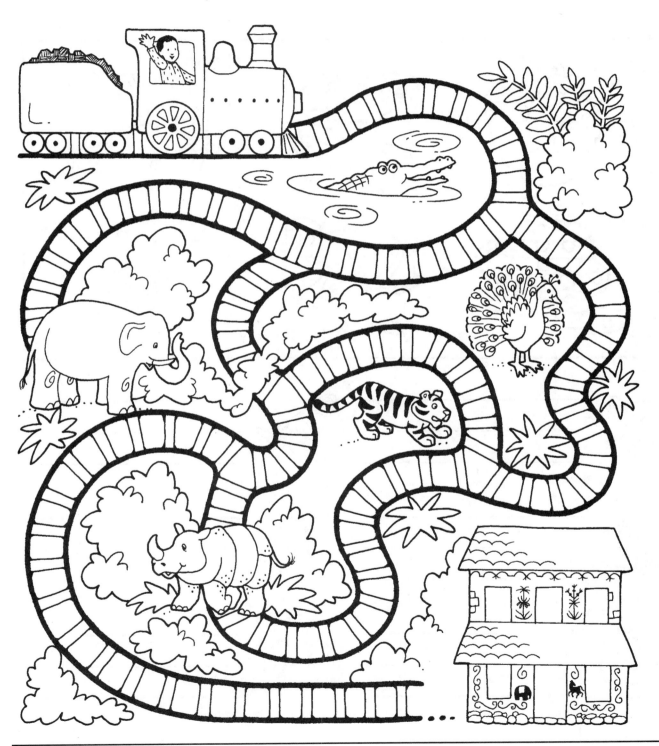

Daily Learning Drills Grade K

Name _____

Rain Forest Animals

Look at the picture. Read the words. Write the words on the lines.

sloth

frog

tiger

snake

monkey

bird

 _____

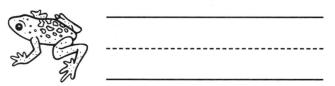 _____

 _____

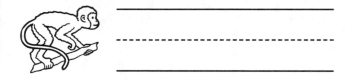 _____

Name _____

A Warm, Wet Forest

A rain forest is warm. Rain falls most days.
The rain forest is always green.

Color the trees and plants green.
Then draw falling rain. Color
the animals.

SCIENCE

Name _____

What's Wrong?

In each picture, cross out the part that cannot really happen. Color the pictures.

Name _____

Ocean Home

Color the pictures. Read about ocean habitats.

Some animals live near the shore of the ocean.

Some animals live in very deep ocean waters.

Some animals live near the top of the ocean waters.

Some animals fly above the ocean waters.

Name _____

Ocean Animals

Write each animal's name in the correct place.

Whale	shark
crab	clam
gull	fish

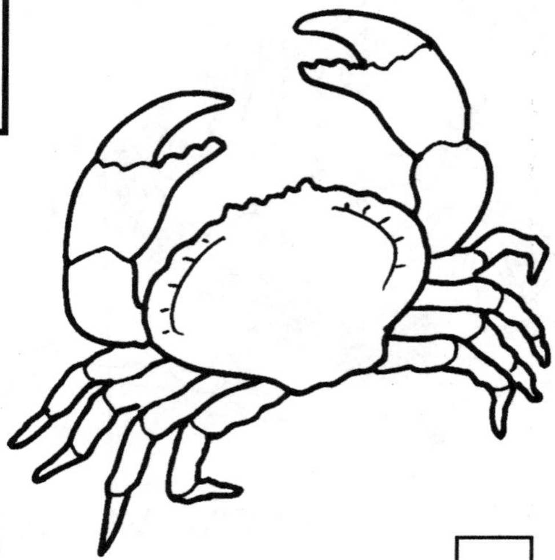

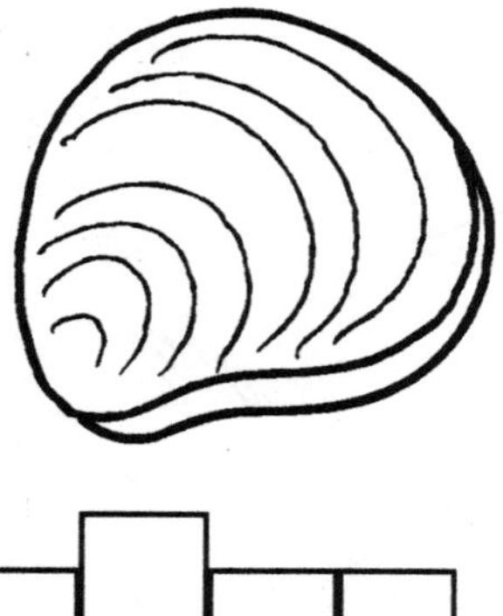

Name _____

Fishy Friends

Help the striped fish swim through the coral and find its friend.

SCIENCE

Name _____

Beautiful Birds

Circle the words. The words go → and ↓.

s	g	p	m	e	b	r	e	t
p	c	a	r	d	i	n	a	l
a	r	r	d	o	r	o	g	c
r	n	r	a	s	t	u	l	h
r	i	o	w	o	w	l	e	m
o	x	t	l	y	k	f	p	l
w	d	v	f	r	o	b	i	n

 sparrow    cardinal

 parrot   owl

 robin   eagle

Name _____

Spiders

Color. Read about spiders.

Spiders are not insects.
Insects have six legs.
Spiders have eight legs.

Spiders spin sticky webs
to make homes and
to catch food.

Insects get stuck in
the webs. The spiders
spin silk around the insects
and eat them for dinner!

Name _____

A Bunch of Butterflies

Color the butterfly that is different.

Name _____

Go Buggy!

Unscramble each word. Use the Word Bank for help. Write the words in the puzzle.

Word Bank

wasp

moth

bee

ant

grasshopper

mosquito

butterfly

cricket

Down

1. rkctice
2. ebe
3. omht

Across

4. paws
5. ytebrutlf
6. oqistomu
7. psogsrphaer
8. tna

Name _____

Bug Walk

Show the bug how to cross the leaf.

Name _____

A Bunch of Beetles

Find the **3** beetles that match. Color them.

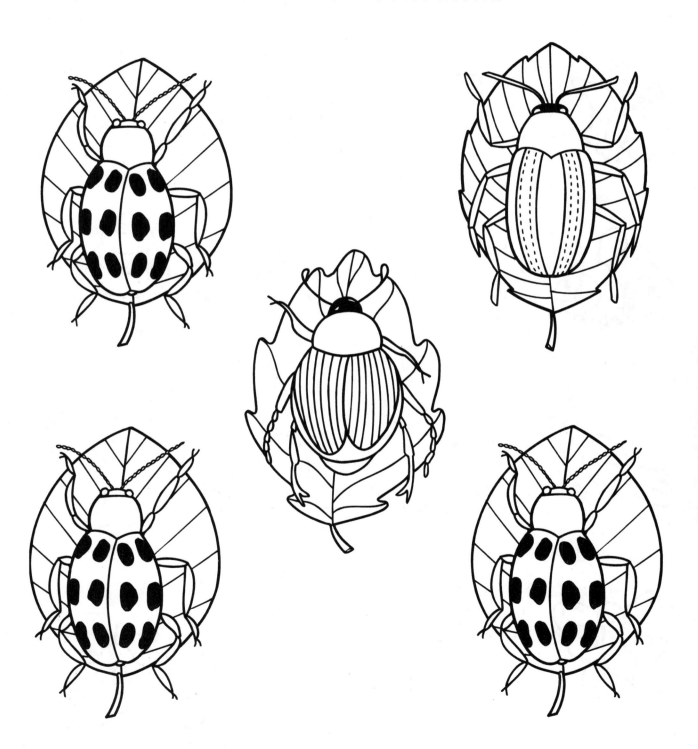

Daily Learning Drills Grade K

Name _____

Where Is My Home?

Trace each path. Color the pictures.

Name _____

Animal Sightings

Cut out each animal card below on the dotted lines. Glue each card under the picture of where you find the animal.

water	land	sky

camel 	owl	dolphin
lion 	parrot 	elephant
whale 	zebra	goose

SCIENCE

Name _____

A Long Time Ago

Color the scene. Then trace the letters below.

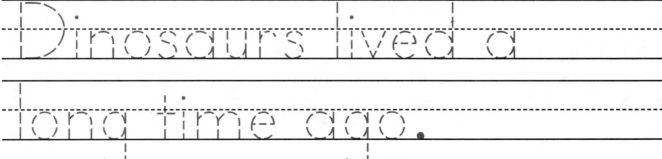

Dinosaurs lived a
long time ago.

Daily Learning Drills Grade K

SCIENCE

Name _____

Maiasaura Maze

Some dinosaurs made nests on the ground. They laid eggs in the nests. Baby dinosaurs hatched from the eggs.

Can you help Mother Maiasaura get back to her nest? Draw a line to show her path. Watch out! T-Rex wants to eat her.

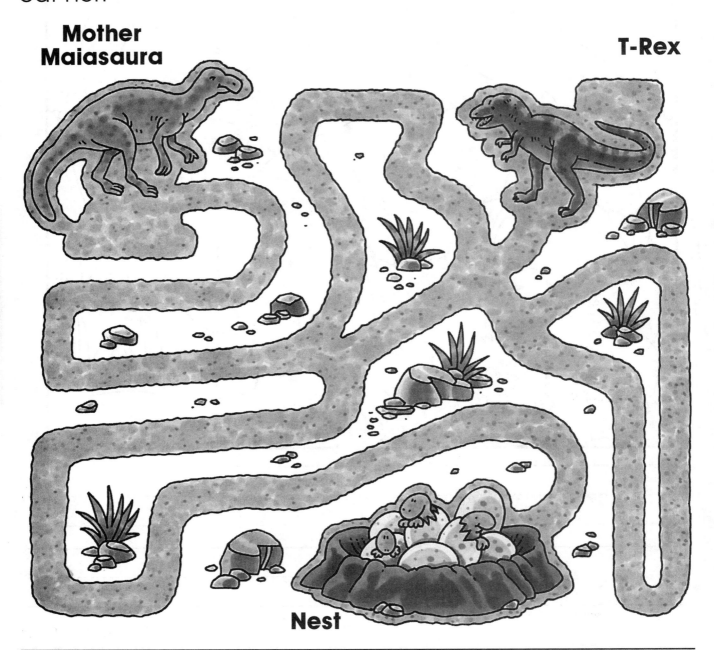

Name _____

Long Gone

Connect the dots from **1** to **25**. Color.

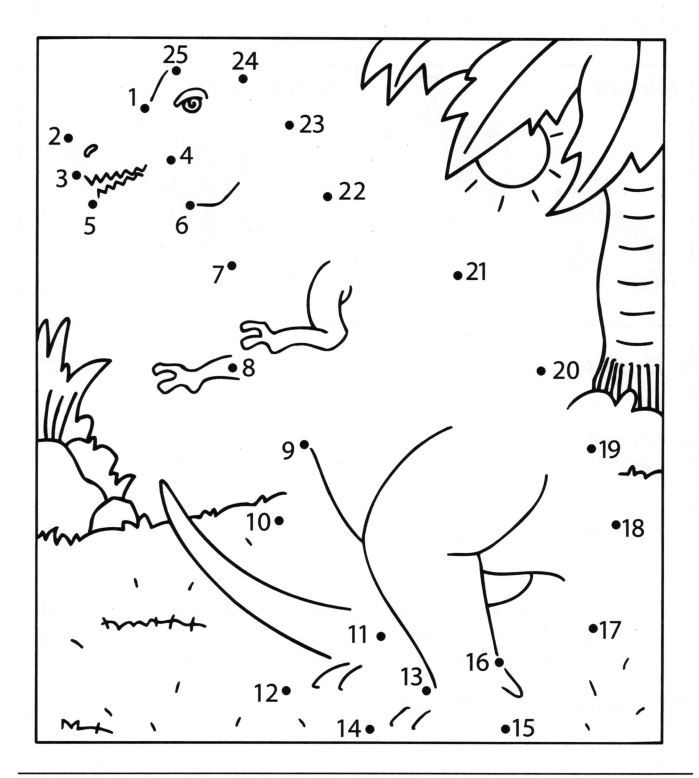

SCIENCE

Name _____

Plant-Eater or Meat-Eater?

Some dinosaurs ate meat. Some dinosaurs ate plants. Look at the pictures. Circle yes or no to answer the questions.

Allosaurus

Apatosaurus

1. Does it have sharp teeth?	1. Does it have sharp teeth?
yes no	yes no
2. Does it stand upright on two strong back legs?	2. Does it stand upright on two strong back legs?
yes no	yes no
3. Does it have claws?	3. Does it have claws?
yes no	yes no
If the answers are yes, circle meat-eater. If the answers are no, circle plant-eater.	If the answers are yes, circle meat-eater. If the answers are no, circle plant-eater.
meat-eater plant-eater	meat-eater plant-eater

Name _____

Seasons

Color the pictures. Trace and say the season words.

winter

spring

summer

fall

Daily Learning Drills Grade K

Name _____

Spring, Summer, Fall, Winter

Number the events in order. Write a number in each box. Then color the pictures.

Name _____

Fall Scramble

Unscramble the fall word on each leaf. Color the leaf the correct color.

aotc

_ _ _ _

red

ndwi

_ _ _ _

blue

oancr

_ _ _ _ _

purple

eter

_ _ _ _

green

aleevs

_ _ _ _ _ _

brown

lbotaofl

_ _ _ _ _ _ _ _

orange

aerk

_ _ _ _

yellow

ohoslc

_ _ _ _ _ _

black

acorn   coat
football   rake
school   tree
wind   leaves

Name _____

Winter Word Search

Circle each winter word from the word box in the puzzle. Check off each word as you find it. Words go across and down.

☐ flakes   ☐ blizzard   ☐ sled   ☐ cold

☐ skate   ☐ snow   ☐ snowman   ☐ freeze

☐ January   ☐ ice   ☐ mittens   ☐ ski

r	f	r	a	m	k	l	i	n	x
s	l	e	d	n	f	k	c	k	v
J	a	n	u	a	r	y	e	i	c
s	k	a	t	e	e	b	g	s	o
n	e	g	f	t	e	t	s	g	l
o	s	b	l	i	z	z	a	r	d
w	m	i	t	t	e	n	s	s	r
b	i	m	s	k	i	y	o	k	o
s	n	o	w	m	a	n	g	y	v

Name _____

How Is the Weather?

Trace and color.

_____
sunny

_____
cloudy

_____
rainy

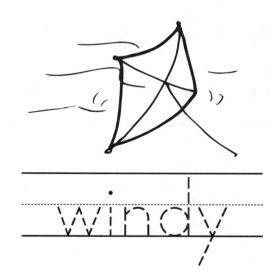

_____
windy

How is the weather today?

_____

_____ .

Name _____

Weather Words

Circle the words. The words go → and ↓.

f	r	d	l	w	i	n	d	y
z	a	r	i	a	o	c	w	b
r	i	u	t	b	t	l	g	s
s	n	o	w	y	s	o	y	u
u	y	s	a	n	q	u	j	n
x	k	p	r	n	w	d	e	n
h	c	v	m	i	n	y	m	y

 warm

 rainy

 sunny

 snowy

 cloudy

 windy

Name _____

Cold or Warm?

Look at the clothes each child is wearing.
Circle **cold** if the child is dressed for cold weather.
Circle **warm** if the child is dressed for warm weather.

cold   warm

cold   warm

cold   warm

cold   warm

cold   warm

cold   warm

SCIENCE

Name _____

How Does It Feel Outside?

Write a word for each picture.

hot	warm	cold

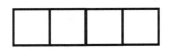

How does it feel outside today?

_____

- -

_____

Name _____

Rain or Shine

Look at each weather forecast on the left and draw a line to show what the girl should wear.

Name _____

Off to Space!

Connect the dots from **1** to **25**. Color to finish the picture.

Name _____

Far Out!

Circle the words. The words go → and ↓.

e	s	r	i	o	r	b	i	t
o	p	l	p	k	d	v	g	r
x	a	t	l	e	h	m	j	o
m	c	w	a	f	i	o	r	c
y	e	s	n	t	n	o	c	k
b	k	h	e	y	p	n	f	e
s	h	u	t	t	l	e	y	t

 rocket

 moon

 space

 orbit

 planet

 shuttle

Daily Learning Drills Grade K

Name _____

My Name

Write your name.

First name

_____

- -

_____

Middle name

_____

- -

_____

Last name

_____

- -

_____

Name _____

Baby Days

Draw a picture of yourself when you were a baby.

Circle.

I was born on a _____.

Monday   Tuesday   Wednesday
Thursday   Friday   Saturday   Sunday

I am the _____ child in my family.

first   second   third   fourth   fifth

Name _____

Happy Birthday

Draw candles to show how old you are.

_____

I am _____ years old.

My birthday is

_____

_____ .

Name _____

Look What I Can Do!

Put a ✓ in the box if you do the activity each day.

Eat		
Get dressed		
Brush teeth		
Take a bath		
Go to school		
Play		
Read books		
Watch TV		
Go to bed		

SOCIAL STUDIES

Getting Bigger Each Day

Color the things that you can do now. Circle the things that you want to learn to do. Continue on the next page.

Name _____

Daily Learning Drills Grade K

SOCIAL STUDIES

Name _____

Things I Like to Do

Say the words.
Color the pictures of the things you like to do.

jump

sing

cook

write

skip

swim

Name _____

My Favorite Toy

Draw a picture of your favorite toy.

Color other toys you like.

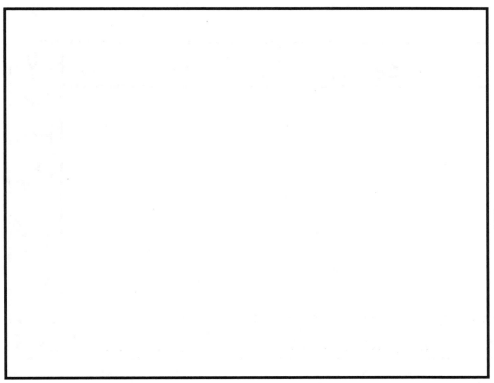

Daily Learning Drills Grade K

SOCIAL STUDIES

Name _____

My Family Laughs!

Draw a picture showing something that makes your family laugh.

Color the things that make you laugh.

Name _____

I Can Get Mad

Color the pictures that make you feel mad.

Daily Learning Drills Grade K

SOCIAL STUDIES

Name _____

I Get Scared

Color the pictures of things that scare you.

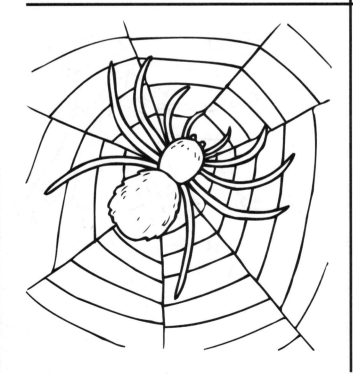

Name _____

My Family

Trace the words. Draw a picture of your family.

father   sister   mother

grandmother

brother   grandfather

Name _____

We Do Things Together

Look at each picture. If your family likes to do what is shown, color the picture.

Name _____

Daily Learning Drills Grade K

SOCIAL STUDIES

Name _____

My Jobs

Color the pictures of the jobs you do.

Name _____

When I Am Older

Color the pictures of the jobs that you would like to
do someday.

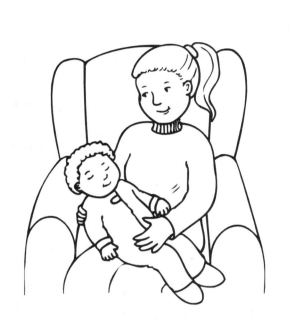

SOCIAL STUDIES

Name _____

I Play Inside

Color the things you could play with inside.
Draw an X on the things you could not play with inside.

Name _____

Indoor and Outdoor Fun

Color the things you use inside yellow. Color the things you use outside blue.

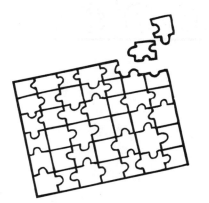

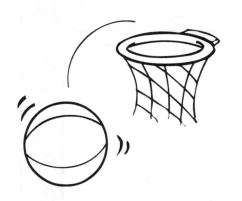
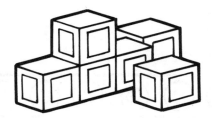

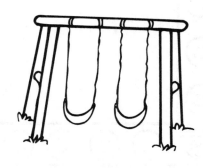

SOCIAL STUDIES

Name _____

My Friends

Draw a picture of two of your friends.

My friends' names are _____

_____

and _____

_____

We like to _____

Name _____

Friends Are Polite

Look at each picture.
Write the polite sentences next to the matching pictures.

Say this if you ask for something.

Say this if your friend gives you something.

Say this if you hurt your friend's feelings.

Thank you!　　**I'm sorry.**　　**Please.**

SOCIAL STUDIES

Name _____

Friends Have Fun

Draw a line to the picture that completes the sentence.

banana

You may ride my _____.

letter

Have a bite of this _____.

bicycle

You may pet the _____.

ball

I will write you a _____.

cat

I will throw the _____.

Name _____

Chef Charlie

Chef Charlie tossed the pizza crust. Where did it go?

SOCIAL STUDIES

careers

When I Grow Up

Color the pictures that show what you might be when you grow up.

Name _____

When I grow up, I want to be a

_____

- -

_____

SOCIAL STUDIES

Name _____

Learning the Past

Help the museum guide find the dinosaur display.

Name _____

To the Rescue

Connect the dots from **A** to **Z**. Color.

Daily Learning Drills Grade K

Name _____

Places

Draw lines to show where each item belongs.
Say the names of the places.

farm

bed

park bench

park

house

desk

tractor

school

What is your favorite place?

_____

_____

_____

Name _____

A Busy Day

Circle the things that are in the picture.

MAIL

Daily Learning Drills Grade K

SOCIAL STUDIES

Name _____

Off to School

Connect the dots from **A** to **Z**.

Name _____

A Classroom

Finish each sentence with the name of what you see.

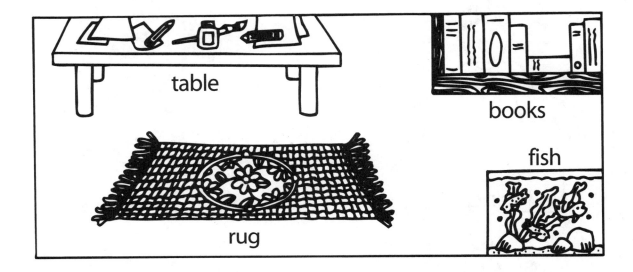

table

books

fish

rug

_____

You will go to the _____ .

_____

You will go to the _____ .

_____

You will go to the _____ .

_____

You will go to the _____ .

SOCIAL STUDIES

Name _____

School Time

Color the pictures. Check off the boxes of the things you do at school.

☐ sing

☐ draw

☐ count

☐ paint

☐ read

☐ write

Name _____

Playground Fun

Trace the words.

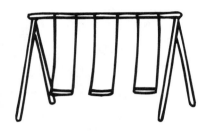

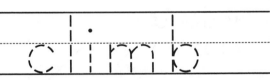

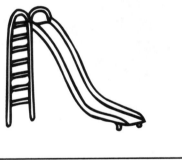

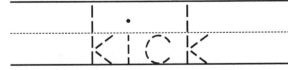

What do you like to do at the playground?

_____

_____

SOCIAL STUDIES

Name _____

Safety Sign Match

Draw a line from each safety sign to its shadow.

railroad
crossing

no
bicycles

school
crossing

bicycle
crossing

stop

Name _____

Workers Use Transportation

Draw lines to match the pictures.

SOCIAL STUDIES

Daily Learning Drills Grade K

Name _____

Words to Know

Look at the picture. Read the words.
Write the words on the lines.

boat

bus

plane

car

bike

truck

Name _____

A Busy Street

Look at the picture. Write **3** things that people ride.

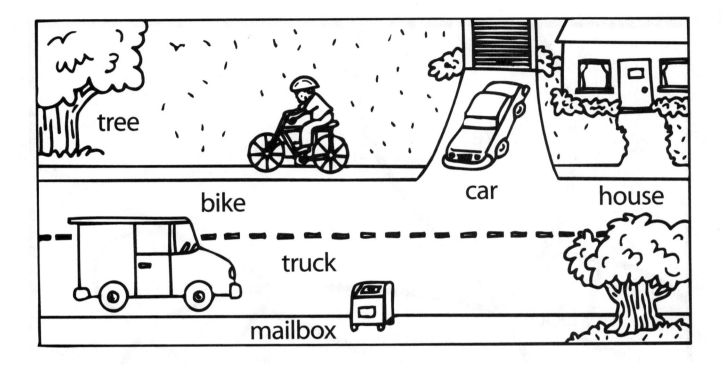

1. _____

2. _____

3. _____

SOCIAL STUDIES

Name _____

Let's Go!

Color the spaces with words for ways to travel.

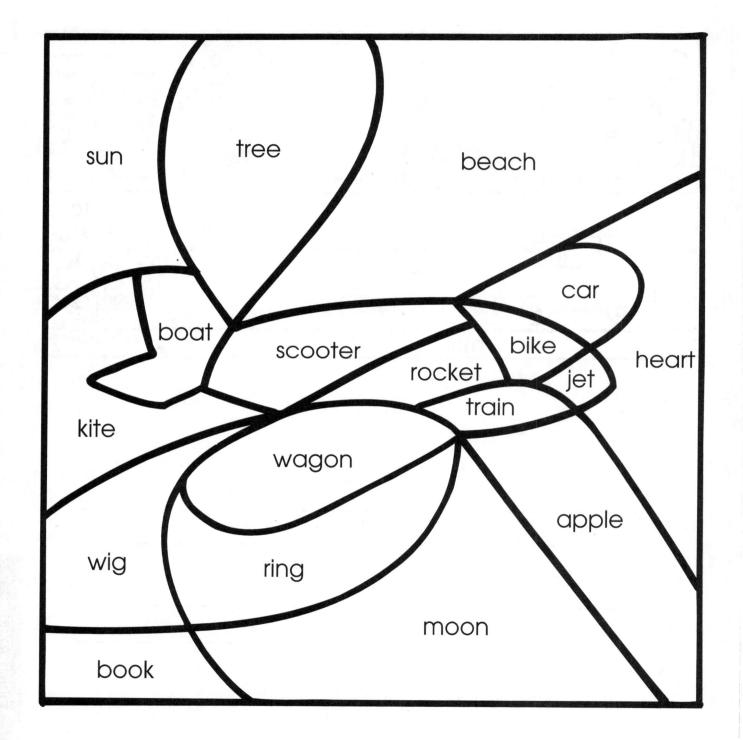

Name _____

Look and Find

Find three kinds of transportation.
Trace each one with a different color.

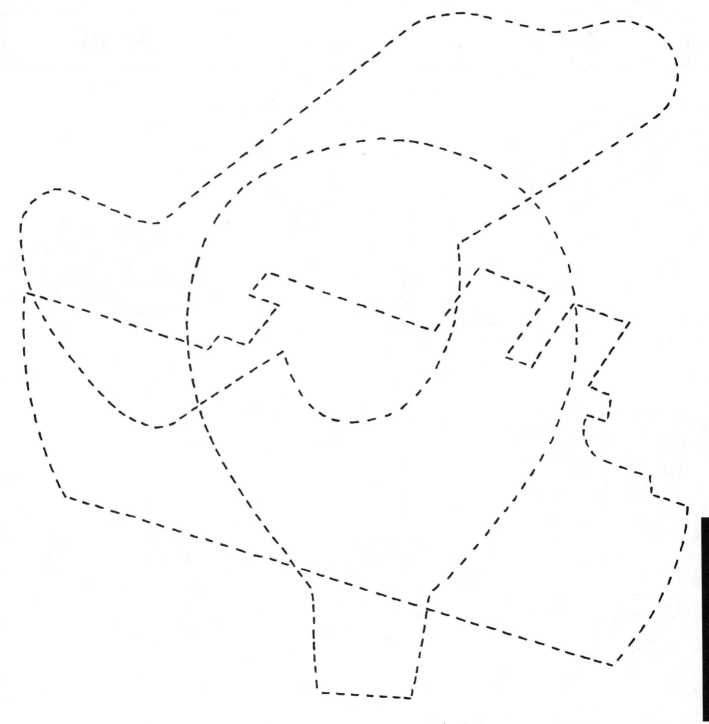

SOCIAL STUDIES

Name _____

On the Go!

Draw a line from each picture to the word that describes what it travels on. Then color the pictures.

air	**water**	**land**

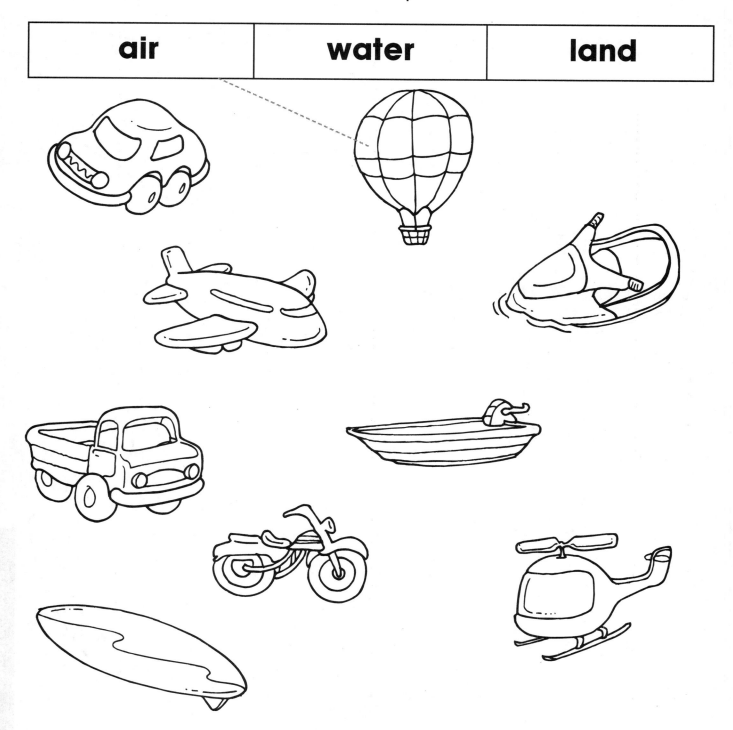

Name _____

Getting There

Check off each kind of transportation you have used.
Draw a circle around a kind of transportation you
would like to try some day.

☐ bicycle   ☐ train   ☐ horse & wagon

☐ ferry   ☐ airplane   ☐ boat

☐ car   ☐ subway   ☐ helicopter

☐ semitrailer   ☐ bus   ☐ camel

☐ streetcar   ☐ snowmobile   ☐ skateboard

Name _____

Going on a Trip

Where would you like to go on a trip? Draw it.
Trace and finish the sentence.

I will go to _____

_____

Name _____

Color the things that you will take on your trip.

Daily Learning Drills Grade K

SOCIAL STUDIES

Name _____

Away We Go

Circle and write the best title for each picture.

The Big Plane

Trains Are Fun

Going to Camp

A Snowy Day

On Our Boat

At the Zoo

Name _____

If I Could Go Anywhere

Draw a picture to show where you would like to visit.

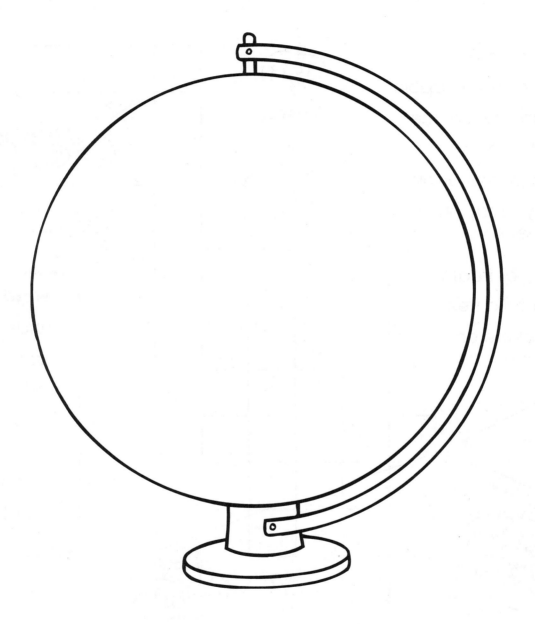

I would like to visit

_____

- -

_____

SOCIAL STUDIES

Name _____

Halloween Puzzle

Read each clue. Write the correct word in the puzzle space.

Down

1. You wear me.

3. I taste good on apples.

4. I spin my own home.

Across

1. I am made of apples.

2. What you say on Halloween is "_____-or-treat"

5. I grow on a tree.

6. You get me on Halloween.

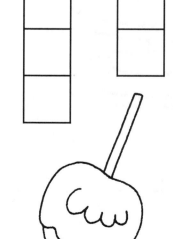

Words

cider

apple

costume

spider

trick

caramel

candy

Name _____

Leprechaun Puppet

On St. Patrick's Day, people wear green and put leprechauns in their windows. Color, cut, and glue pieces on a paper lunch bag. Use for puppet plays.

SOCIAL STUDIES

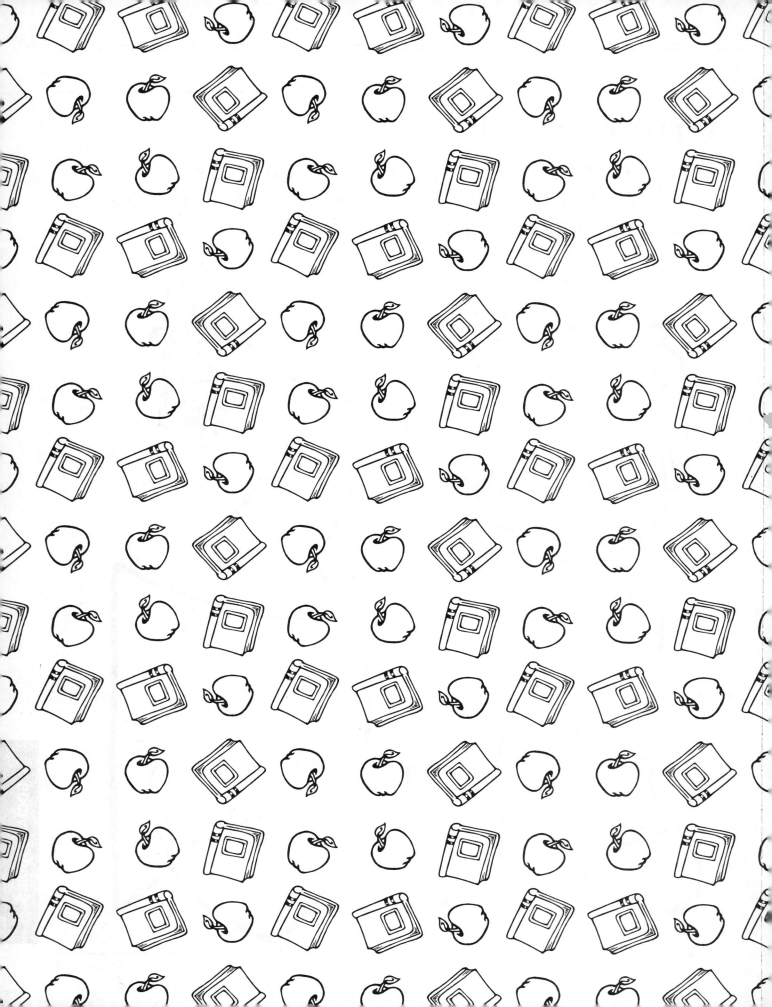

Name _____

Search for Spring Holiday Words

Circle each spring word in the word search.
Check off each word on the list as you find it in the puzzle.
Words go across and down.

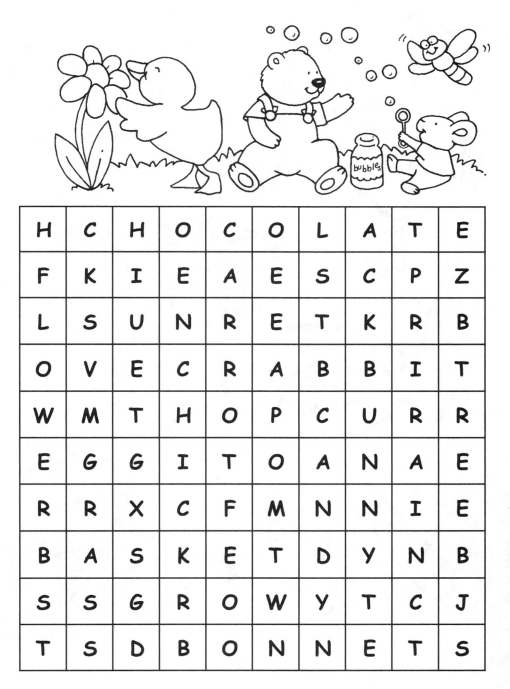

☐	bunny
☐	tree
☐	chocolate
☐	bonnet
☐	carrot
☐	hop
☐	rain
☐	egg
☐	grass
☐	grow
☐	flower
☐	rabbit
☐	chick
☐	basket
☐	candy
☐	sun

H	C	H	O	C	O	L	A	T	E
F	K	I	E	A	E	S	C	P	Z
L	S	U	N	R	E	T	K	R	B
O	V	E	C	R	A	B	B	I	T
W	M	T	H	O	P	C	U	R	R
E	G	G	I	T	O	A	N	A	E
R	R	X	C	F	M	N	N	I	E
B	A	S	K	E	T	D	Y	N	B
S	S	G	R	O	W	Y	T	C	J
T	S	D	B	O	N	N	E	T	S

Daily Learning Drills Grade K

Name _____

A Special Day

Color the pictures that show things your family uses to celebrate a special holiday.

Name _____

My Holiday Dream

Write about a holiday dream.

_____
_____
_____
_____
_____
_____
_____
_____

z-z-z

Daily Learning Drills Grade K

SOCIAL STUDIES

Name _____

Don't Litter

Color the picture of the seashore. Then put a big **X** on all the trash that should go in the trash can. There are five pieces of trash.

Name _____

City or Village Life

Color the pictures that show city life **blue**. Color the pictures that show village live **orange**. Color the pictures that can be village or city live **red**.

Daily Learning Drills Grade K

SOCIAL STUDIES

Name _____

Mountain Maze

One of Maria's chores is collecting reeds for weaving baskets. Help Maria find her way through the mountain trails to get to the river bank where the reeds grow.

Name _____

The Great Wall

The longest structure in the world is in China. It is called the Great Wall. Work your way through the Great Wall maze.

FINISH

Name _____

Chinese Calendar

When is your birthday? _____

In which Chinese year were you born? _____

What is the animal sign
for your Chinese birth year? _____

Color the animals in the calendar.

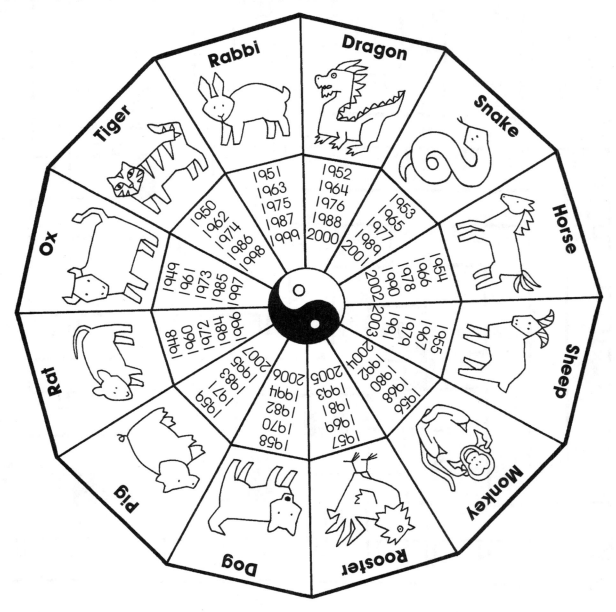

Name _____

Map Activity

1. Draw a star where New Delhi, the capital, is located.
2. Circle Darjeeling.
3. Draw a boat in the Indian Ocean.
4. Draw a snowflake in the Himalayan Mountains.
5. Trace the Ganges River with blue.
6. Write INDIA in the center of the country.

Name _____

The Australian Flag

Color the flag. Use the numbers to help you.

1 = blue   **2 = white**   **3 = red**

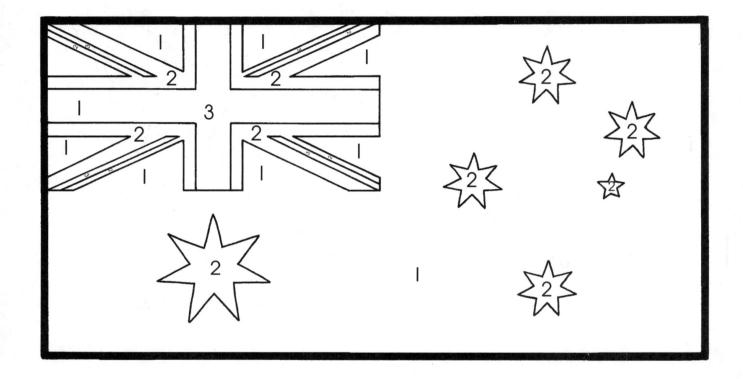

Answer Key

Sailing Away
Connect the dots from **A** to **Z**.

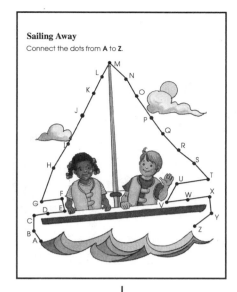

1

Let's Play Leapfrog
Help the girl find her way to the frog exhibit. Color the path in order from **N** to **Z**.

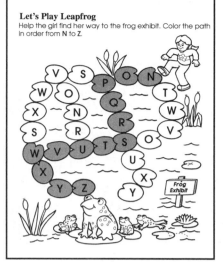

2

Sailing Away
Follow the alphabet to lead the pig to the radio.

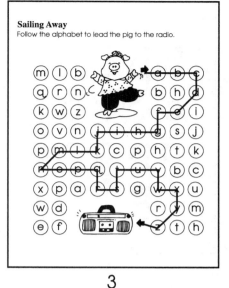

3

Fantastic Farm
Find the letters from **a** to **m**. Color them.

a b c d e f g h i j k l m

4

Trace and Write
Trace the letters. Then write each letter.

5

Trace and Write
Trace the letters. Then write each letter.

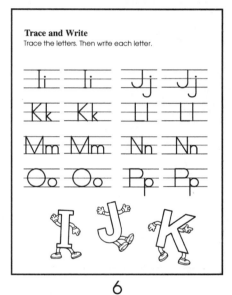

6

Trace and Write
Trace the letters. Then write each letter.

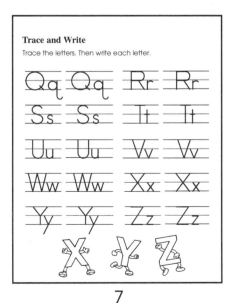

7

Letter Trucks
Write the letter that comes between.

8

Letter Matchup
In each row, circle the letters that match the first letter.

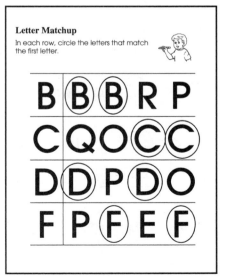

9

Daily Learning Drills Grade K

More Matching

In each row, circle the letters that match the first letter.

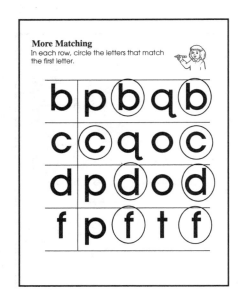

Letter Garden

Draw lines between the flowers to match the uppercase and lowercase letters.

Aa Bb Cc Dd Ee Ff Gg Hh Ii
Jj Kk Ll Mm Nn Oo Pp Qq Rr
Ss Tt Uu Vv Ww Xx Yy Zz

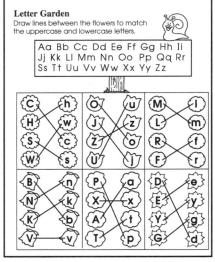

10

I Can Match Letters

Draw a line from each child to the matching lowercase letter.

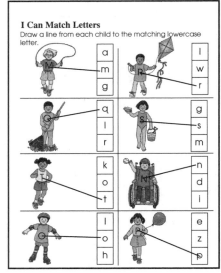

11

12

Follow the Path

Say the alphabet. Write the missing letters.

A Lost Ball

Help Tommy find his ball.
Follow the words in ABC order.

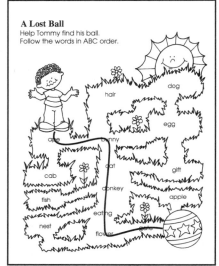

Hungry Birds

Help the birds find the worms.
Color the boxes in ABC order.

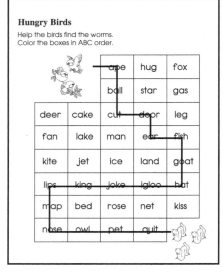

13

14

15

New Word Fun

Write the first letter for each picture.
Write the letters in the boxes to make a new word.

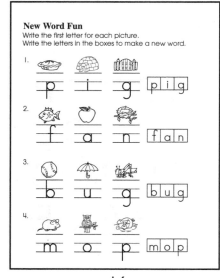

Fill Them In

Write the vowels to complete each word.

The Sound of C

Draw a line from each cat to a picture that begins with the sound of **c**.

Write **Cc**.

16

17

18

The Sound of G

Color the pictures that begin with the sound of **g**.

Write **Gg**.

Gg Gg Gg Gg Gg

19

The Sound of L

Look at the living room. Draw a circle around five things that begin with the sound of **L**. Color the picture.

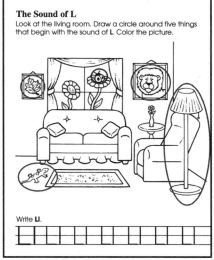

Write **Ll**.

20

Rain, Rain, Go Away

Find these things, which begin with **m**. Color them brown. Then color the rest of the picture.

mouse   monkey   mop   milk   mask

21

Water Lover

Find these things, which begin with **r**. Color them orange. Then color the rest of the picture

rose   rake   ring   rocket   raccoon

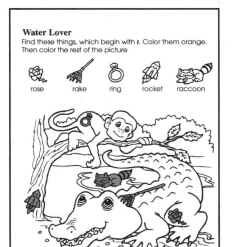

22

Plump Pig

Color each **u** purple. Then color the rest of the picture.

23

The Sound of Y

Look at each picture. If it begins with **y**, circle **yes**. If it does not, circle **no**.

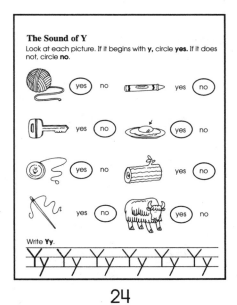

yes   no   yes   no

yes   no   yes   no

yes   no   yes   no

yes   no   yes   no

Write **Yy**.

Yy Yy Yy Yy Yy Yy

24

All Kinds of Animals

Look at each animal. Say its name. Circle the sound you hear at the beginning of the word.

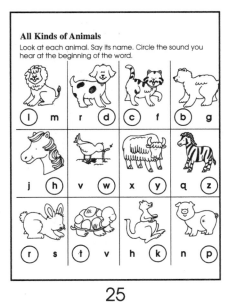

l   m   r   d   c   f   b   g

j   h   v   w   x   y   q   z

r   s   t   v   h   k   n   p

25

Food Fun

Look at the first picture in each row. Say its name. Then color the picture that has the same beginning sound.

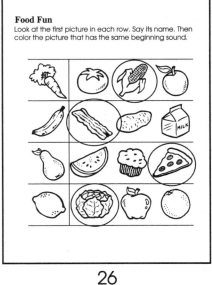

26

Listen Carefully

Look at each column. Color the pictures that begin with the letter shown at the top.

27

Daily Learning Drills Grade K

Matching Sounds
Draw lines from each letter to the pictures with the same beginning sound.

Floating High
Color the words that start with **e** orange.
Color the words that start with **f** yellow.
Write the words under the correct beginning letters below.

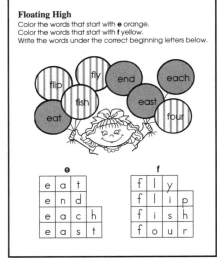

e	a	t
e	n	d
e	a	c	h
e	a	s	t

f	l	y
f	l	i	p
f	i	s	h
f	o	u	r

Scrambled J's, K's, and L's
Unscramble the words that name the pictures. Write the words.

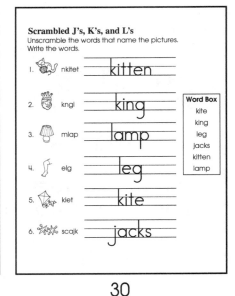

1. nkitet — kitten
2. kngi — king
3. mlap — lamp
4. elg — leg
5. kiet — kite
6. scajk — jacks

Word Box
kite
king
leg
jacks
kitten
lamp

28   29   30

Ending Sounds
Listen for the ending sound of each picture. Write it at the end of each word.

bag   bus

cup

hen   mud

More Ending Sounds
Listen for the ending sound of each picture. Write it at the end of each word.

tub   bed

fan   cat

top   pig

Beginning and End
Say the names of the pictures. Write the letters that make the beginning and ending sounds.

cat   dog

fan   mop

bed   sun

31   32   33

Discovering Differences
Circle the animal that is different in each column.

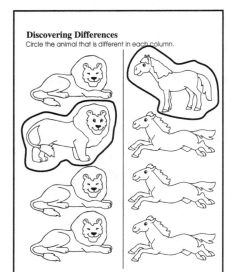

Missing Parts
Some of these elephants are missing body parts! Look at elephant **A** to see what's missing on the others. Name the missing body parts and draw them on the animals.

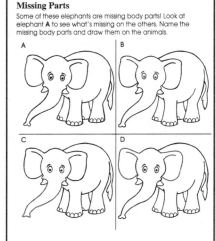

Parts and Wholes
Complete each picture by drawing the missing piece.

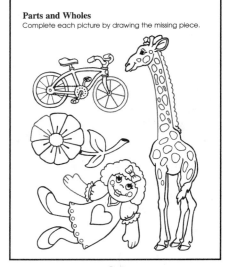

34   35   36

What's Different?

Can you find and circle ten ways the bottom picture is different?

37

Opposite Matchup

Draw lines to match the opposites.

38

Ocean Opposites

Draw lines to match the opposites.

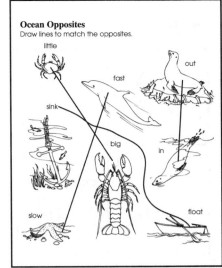

39

Word Match

Match each word with a picture.

cat
dog
pan
ball

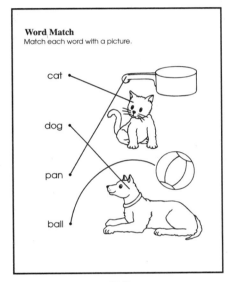

40

Fun Word Match

Match each word with a picture.

plane
leaf
bed
nut

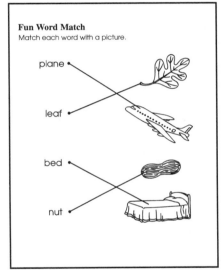

41

Matching Words

Circle matching pairs of words.

go go	sat cat
fox fox	at to
top toe	red red
no no	car cat

42

I Read Words

In each box, circle the words that match the word at the top.

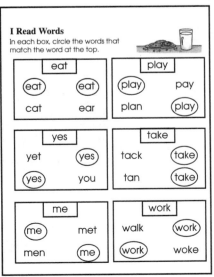

eat	play
eat eat	play pay
cat ear	plan play

yes	take
yet yes	tack take
yes you	tan take

me	work
me met	walk work
men me	work woke

43

Final Question

Match the scrambled letters to find out what the farmer wants to ask.

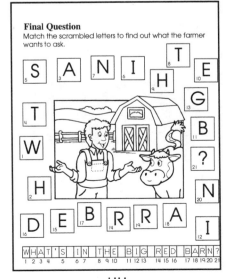

S A N I T E
T H G
W B
H ?
D E B R R A I N

WHAT'S IN THE BIG RED BARN?

44

A Plane

Write the sentence.

See the plane go up.

See the plane go up.

Find and circle the words. The words go across → and down ↓.

Word Box
up
plane
See
go
the

g	S	e	e	n	p
h	l	s	t	v	l
q	g	z	f	r	a
b	o	m	e	c	n
z	r	k	u	p	e
t	h	e	z	o	w

45

293

Daily Learning Drills Grade K

Word Match

Circle the words that match the words at the top of each box.

red sled	fun ride
red slide	fun ride
(red sled)	fan ride

wet kid	hot fire
well kid	(hot fire)
(wet kid)	hot find

46

A Secret Sentence

Color the following words in the puzzle **green**.

camp when test time

How **camp**
old **test**
are **when**
time you

Write the words you did not color to make a sentence.

How old are you ?

47

Look and Color

Color the following words red.

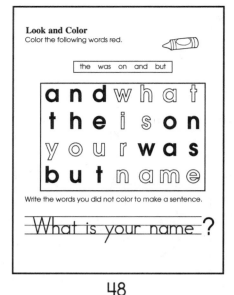

the was on and but

and w h a t
the i s o n
y o u r **was**
but n a m e

Write the words you did not color to make a sentence.

What is your name ?

48

New Words

Color the picture. Add the letter. Write the word.

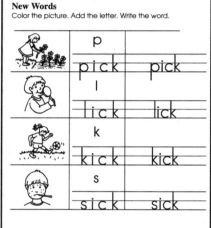

p	
pick	pick
l	
lick	lick
k	
kick	kick
s	
sick	sick

49

Crack the Code

Write the missing letters for each word.
Use the code at the bottom of the page.

1. c r ayon
2. mou s e
3. m oon
4. s ta r
5. c lou d
6. ca r r ot
7. bi r d
8. m on k ey

c	○
r	☆
s	△
m	⬠
d	☐
k	◇

50

Double Trouble

Write each word in the box next to a word in the puzzle to make a new word.

bell	walk	ground	room
box	ball	fish	print

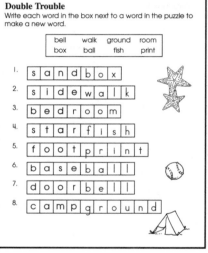

1. s a n d b o x
2. s i d e w a l k
3. b e d r o o m
4. s t a r f i s h
5. f o o t p r i n t
6. b a s e b a l l
7. d o o r b e l l
8. c a m p g r o u n d

51

Figure Them Out

Unscramble each word. Be sure that it matches the meaning.

teacher	ice cream	apple
mouse	jogger	tennis

1. Someone who runs is called a
   riggeo j o g g e r .
2. A game that uses a racket and a small ball is
   stinne t e n n i s .
3. Something cold to eat on a hot day is
   cie ramec i c e   c r e a m .
4. Someone who teaches children is a
   erhteac t e a c h e r .
5. A tasty fruit that grows on a tree is called an
   leppa a p p l e .
6. A furry little animal that squeaks is a
   somue m o u s e .

52

At the Bus Stop

Read each question. Answer the question aloud.
Trace the question mark at the end of the question.

Why are the people waiting?

Who has groceries?

Who has a newspaper?

How many kids are waiting?

53

Is It a Question?

Read the sentence. Then repeat it. After repeating the sentence, tell whether it is a question or a statement.

1. My wagon is red. statement
2. The sky looks cloudy. statement
3. My favorite colors are red and blue. statement
4. Do you know where the store is? question
5. Is this a difficult activity? question
6. I am very tired today. statement
7. First I wake up and then I brush my teeth. statement
8. After school I like to play with my friends. statement
9. What time do you go to school? question
10. He helped her ride the bike last Saturday. statement

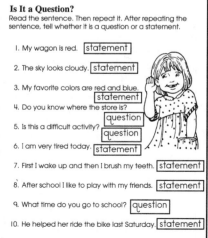

54

Words
Write the correct word on each line.

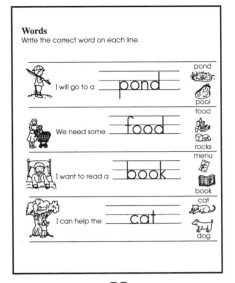

I will go to a ___pond___ — pond / pool

We need some ___food___ — food / rocks

I want to read a ___book___ — menu / book

I can help the ___cat___ — cat / dog

Color Craze
Follow the directions for each coloring activity.

1. Color the items you can eat.

2. Color the objects you write with.

3. Color the toys.

4. Color the fruit.

5. Color the capital letters.

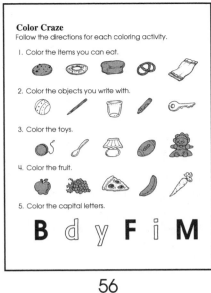

B d y **F** i **M**

55

I Can Have Fun
Color the things that go together in each row.

57

In the Middle
Color each object that is in the middle.

58

Top, Middle, Bottom
Look at the picture. Who is at the **top** of the hill? Who is at the **middle** of the hill? Who is at the **bottom** of the hill? Fill in the blanks below.

The dog is at the ___top___ of the hill.

The cat is at the ___middle___ of the hill.

The boy is at the ___bottom___ of the hill.

59

In or Out
Look at each picture. Circle whether the clown is **in** or **out**.

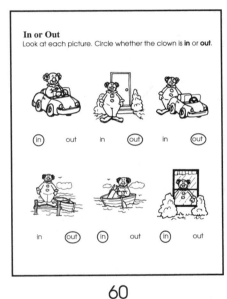

in · out · in · out · in · out

in · out · in · out · in · out

60

More Color Words
Trace the words. Say the color names.
Color the crayons.

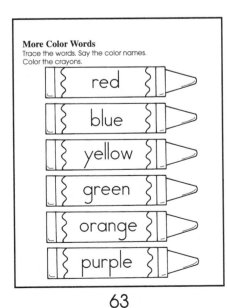

red
blue
yellow
green
orange
purple

63

A Tisket, a Tasket
Follow the directions to color the basket.
1. Color one flower red.
2. Color one flower blue.
3. Draw a bow on the basket.
4. Color the basket green and yellow.
5. Draw another flower in the basket.

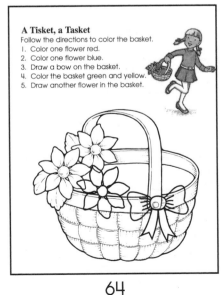

64

Make a Picture
Follow the directions to complete the picture.

1. Draw a tree to the right of the school.

2. Draw a sun in the top left of the picture.

3. Draw a flag to the left of the school.

4. Draw some flowers to the right of the tree.

5. Draw a picture of yourself to the left of the school.

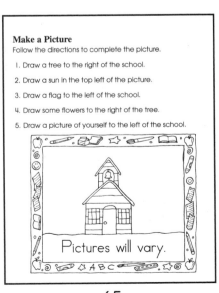

Pictures will vary.

65

Daily Learning Drills Grade K

I Enjoy Books
Circle and write the best title for the picture.

Eating Dinner

Books for Sale

(We Like to Read)

We Like to Read
_____
_____

Can It Really Happen?
Does each picture show something that can really happen?
Circle **yes** if it does.
Circle **no** if it does not.

yes
no

yes
no

yes
no

yes
no

yes
no

yes
no

Funny Garden
Does each picture show something that can really happen?
Circle **yes** if it does.
Circle **no** if it does not.

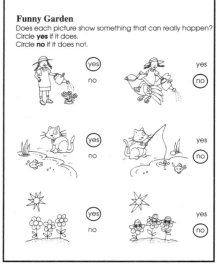

yes
no

yes
no

yes
no

yes
no

yes
no

yes
no

66

67

68

Rhyme Time
Color. Draw lines to match the rhyming words.

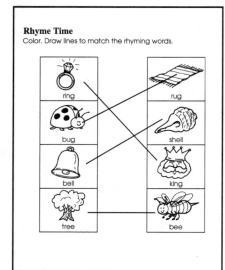

ring   rug

bug   shell

bell   king

tree   bee

Time to Rhyme
Use the picture clues to match the rhyming words.

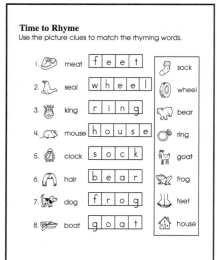

1. meat | f e e t | sock
2. seal | w h e e l | wheel
3. king | r i n g | bear
4. mouse | h o u s e | ring
5. clock | s o c k | goat
6. hair | b e a r | frog
7. dog | f r o g | feet
8. boat | g o a t | house

Before and After
Look at the picture in the middle. Draw something that happens before and after. Trace the words.

before   Answers will vary.

after

69

70

71

Draw a Dinosaur
These pictures are out of order. Number the steps from 1 to 6.

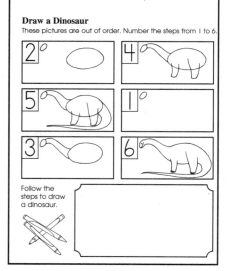

2   4
5   1
3   6

Follow the steps to draw a dinosaur.

My Day at Kindergarten
Read the story below. Then cut out and place the sentences in sequential order.

When the bell rings it is time to go inside. First, the teacher reads a story. Then we have a snack. Finally, we do an art project. At 12:00, it is time to go home.

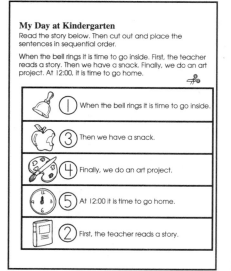

① When the bell rings it is time to go inside.

③ Then we have a snack.

④ Finally, we do an art project.

⑤ At 12:00 it is time to go home.

② First, the teacher reads a story.

Sailing Fun
Listen to a story about Matt and his dad.

Matt and his dad enjoy sailing. When they sail, they like to listen to music. Matt likes fast, loud music. His dad likes slow, soft music. Matt and his dad have lunch on the boat, too. Matt likes hot dogs. His dad likes ham sandwiches.

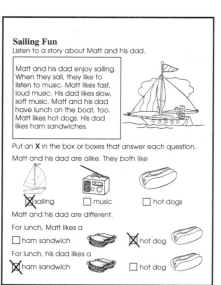

Put an **X** in the box or boxes that answer each question.

Matt and his dad are alike. They both like

☒ sailing   ☐ music   ☐ hot dogs

Matt and his dad are different.

For lunch, Matt likes a
☐ ham sandwich   ☒ hot dog

For lunch, his dad likes a
☒ ham sandwich   ☐ hot dog

72

73

75

Daily Learning Drills Grade K

296

What Happens Next
Draw a line to match the cause to the effect.

Cause   Effect

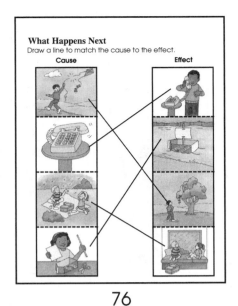

76

I Can Circle What Happens Next
Circle the picture that shows what will happen next.

Daniel threw a stick across the yard for his dog, Muffy. | Muffy will take a nap. | Muffy will run to get the stick.

Rachel wrote a letter. She put it in an envelope and put a stamp on it. | Rachel will put the letter in the mailbox. | Rachel will put the letter in the bathtub.

The cake was cool. Tyler got the bowl of frosting. | Tyler will cut the cake. | Tyler will frost the cake.

77

Size Search
Cut out the animal cards below. Glue each animal under the correct size.

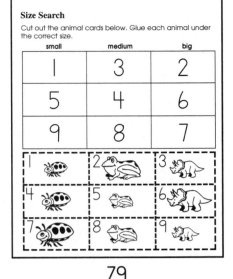

small	medium	big
1	3	2
5	4	6
9	8	7

79

The Pick of the Garden
Circle the animal that is biggest in each row.

Robin   Grasshopper   Beetle

Butterfly   Rabbit   Snail

Caterpillar   Hummingbird   Squirrel

80

Perfectly Pleasing Patterns
Circle the object that comes next. Color the pictures.

81

Grow a Garden
Circle the item that comes next in each row.

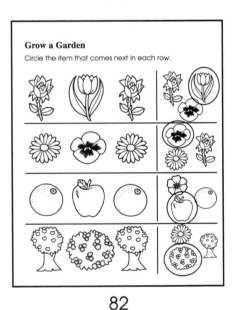

82

Animal Parade
Circle the animal that comes next in each parade.

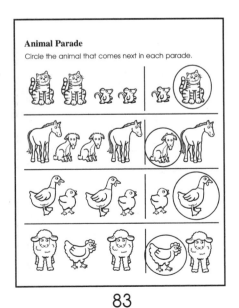

83

Drawing Shapes

Trace.	Draw.	Trace.	Draw.

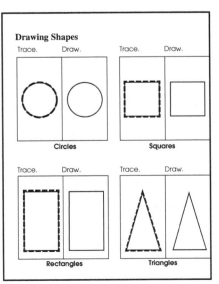

Circles   Squares

Rectangles   Triangles

84

Floating Up
Color **6** ◯ orange.
Color **7** ☆ blue.

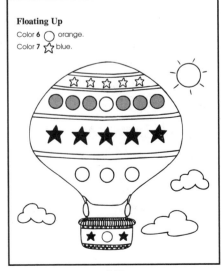

85

Shape Words

Trace and say the shape word. Draw lines to match the shape word to the object.

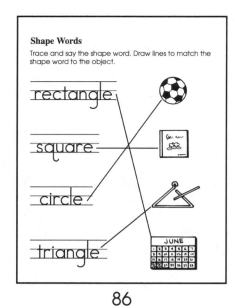

rectangle

square

circle

triangle

Other Shapes

Trace and draw.

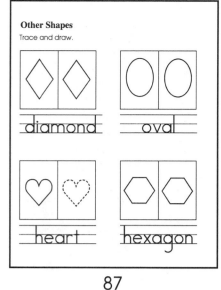

diamond oval

heart hexagon

Fun on the Farm

Find the circles, triangles, and squares. Color them. Color the rest of the picture.

86 87 88

Matching Shapes

Look at each row. Say the shape name. Color the objects that have the same shape.

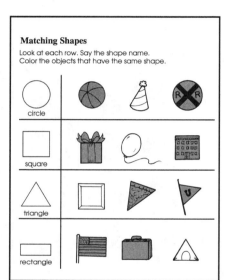

circle

square

triangle

rectangle

A Yummy Number

To find the mystery number, color the spaces with these numbers purple.

9 5 8 7 10 13 18 17 20 19 11

Circle the mystery number. ⑤ 10 18

Water Wonder

Color to find the hidden picture.

5 = yellow **7** = green **10** = blue

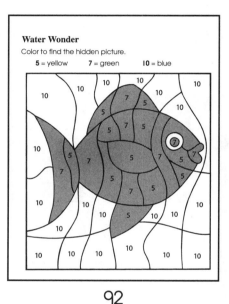

89 91 92

Polly Want a Cracker?

Color to find the hidden picture.

13 = green **14** = orange **15** = yellow

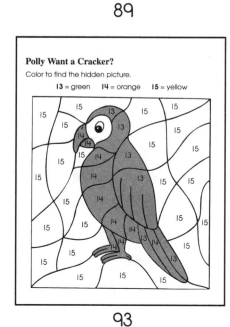

Floating Away

Color to find the hidden picture.

18 = blue **19** = red **20** = yellow

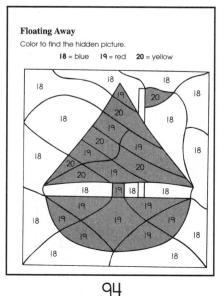

Count and Write

Trace the numbers.

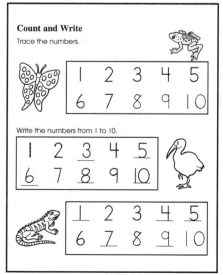

1 2 3 4 5
6 7 8 9 10

Write the numbers from 1 to 10.

1 2 3 4 5
6 7 8 9 10

1 2 3 4 5
6 7 8 9 10

93 94 95

Let's Count

Write the missing numbers.

96

Number Connector

Connect the number words in order. Then color the number you made.

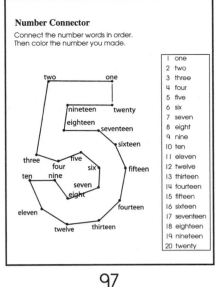

1	one
2	two
3	three
4	four
5	five
6	six
7	seven
8	eight
9	nine
10	ten
11	eleven
12	twelve
13	thirteen
14	fourteen
15	fifteen
16	sixteen
17	seventeen
18	eighteen
19	nineteen
20	twenty

97

Count and Match

Count. Draw a line to the correct number word. Trace each number word.

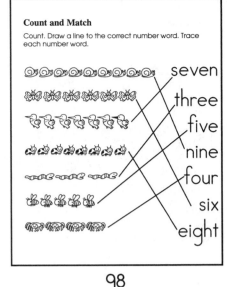

98

Counting Critters

Count the things in each group. Write the number word in the boxes by the pictures.

1 one	2 two	3 three	4 four
5 five	6 six	7 seven	8 eight
9 nine	10 ten	11 eleven	12 twelve

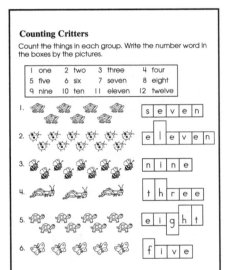

99

Not a Dragon

Connect the dots from 1 to 12. Color to finish the picture.

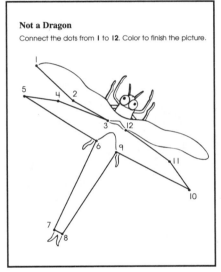

100

Balancing Trick

Connect the dots from 1 to 20. Color to finish the picture.

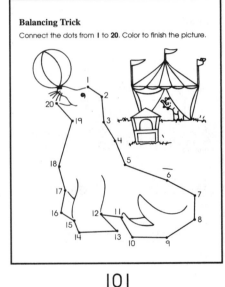

101

In the Town Square

Connect the dots to see what is in the town square.

102

Making Music

Color the sets of 3.

103

Flower Power

Color the sets of 5.

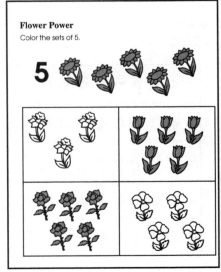

104

Daily Learning Drills Grade K

Mouse Lunch

Find the food and color it green. Then color the rest of the picture.

Circle to show how many.

1 (2) 3   (1) 2   1 (2) 3   1 2 (3)

105

Farm Count

Count the objects. Write the number.

106

Gardening Counting

Count the objects. Write the number.
Circle the smaller number.

107

Barnyard Hoedown

Count the animals and trace the letters below. Color.

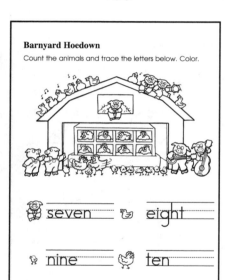

seven   eight

nine   ten

108

Bird Buddies

Find the numbers 1 to 10 in the picture. Color them.

109

I Can Count

Count and color.

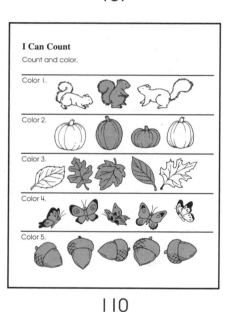

Color 1.

Color 2.

Color 3.

Color 4.

Color 5.

110

It's a Ten

Draw more objects to make ten in each set. Then color the pictures.

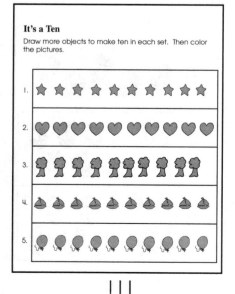

1.

2.

3.

4.

5.

111

Tally It Up

Use tally marks to show how many objects are in each box.

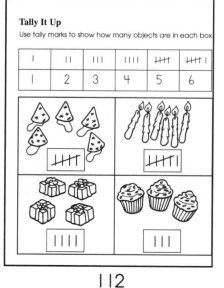

I	II	III	IIII	⊦⊦⊦⊦	⊦⊦⊦⊦ I
1	2	3	4	5	6

112

Count the Objects

Count. Circle the number.

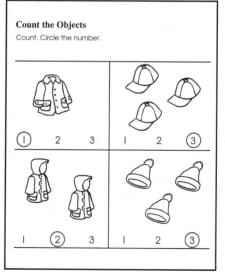

(1) 2 3   1 2 (3)

1 (2) 3   1 2 (3)

113

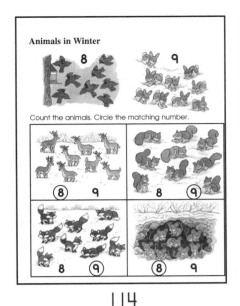

Animals in Winter

8   9

Count the animals. Circle the matching number.

8   9
8   **9**
8   9   **8**   9

114

Super Circles

Count the circles. Color them.

Circle to show how many circles you found.

11   12   13   14   15   16   **17**   18   19   20

115

Spotty Leopards

Circle the number of spots on each leopard.

17   17
18   18
19   **19**

17   **17**
18   18
19   19

116

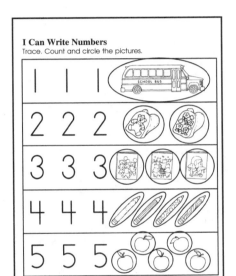

I Can Write Numbers
Trace. Count and circle the pictures.

1 1 1

2 2 2

3 3 3

4 4 4

5 5 5

117

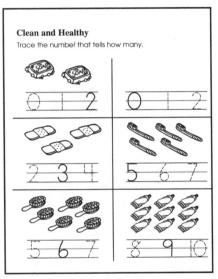

Clean and Healthy

Trace the number that tells how many.

0 1 2   0 1 2

2 3 4   5 6 7

5 6 7   8 9 10

118

Elephant Snacks

Count the peanuts in each bag.
Then write the number on the line.

15   14

16

119

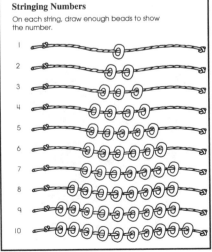

Stringing Numbers

On each string, draw enough beads to show
the number.

1
2
3
4
5
6
7
8
9
10

120

Mouse Hunt

Find **10** mice below. Color them.
Color the rest of the picture.

121

Nut Hunt

Find the nuts . Color them brown. Then color the rest of the picture. Can you find 11 nuts in all?

Big Jumpers!

Find the grasshoppers . Color them green. Then color the rest of the picture. Can you find 12 grasshoppers in all?

Monkeying Around

Find the bananas. Color them yellow. Then color the rest of the picture. Can you find 15 bananas in all?

122

123

124

Color Creations

Find the crayons. Color them purple. Then color the rest of the picture. Can you find 18 crayons in all?

Feeding the Birds

Draw 15 more pieces of birdseed in the bag. Then answer the question below.

How many pieces of birdseed are in the bag now? _20_

Clever Clover

Look carefully at the picture. Find the 25 hidden shamrocks. Color them green.

125

126

127

Fish Bowl

Color 20 fish.

Circle to show how many fish are left over.   (5) 6 7

Snail Garden

Color 25 snails brown 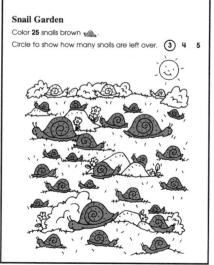.

Circle to show how many snails are left over.   (3) 4 5

128

129

Piggy Bank

Color **24** pennies brown 🪙.

Circle to show how many pennies are left over. 2 ③ 4

Which Is More?

Count the objects in each group. For each row, circle the group with the larger number. Then color the objects.

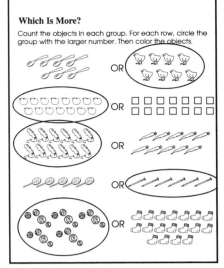

Finding Friends

Help Tommy Turtle find his friends. Color the path that goes in order from **1** to **8**.

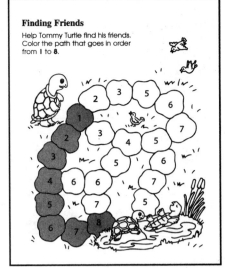

130

131

132

I Can Play

Draw a path to each toy by counting from 1 to 9.

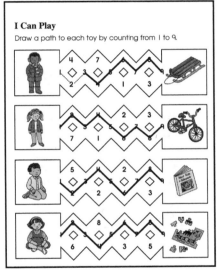

Ready to Land

Count from **1** to **20** to take the plane to the hangar.

A–mazing–ing Football

Get Freddy Football to the end zone by counting by 2s. Starting with 2, color the footballs that contain numbers counting by 2 until you reach the end zone and score a touchdown.

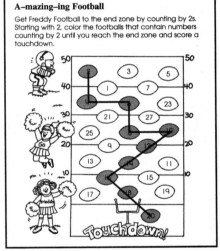

133

134

135

Crazy Counting

Trace. Write the missing numbers.

Count by twos.

2 4 6 8 10

Count by fives.

5 10 15 20 25

Count by tens.

10 20 30 40 50

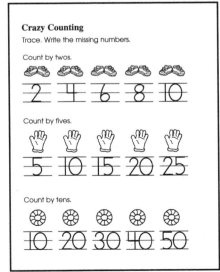

Add them Up

Write the numbers that tell how many.

1 + 1 = 2

1 + 2 = 3

2 + 2 = 4

136

137

Daily Learning Drills Grade K

How Many in All?
Write the numbers that tell how many.

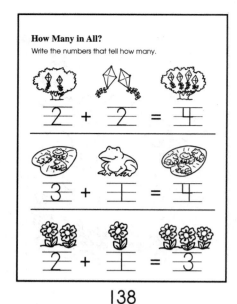

$2 + 2 = 4$

$3 + 1 = 4$

$2 + 1 = 3$

A Special Friend
Add. Then color to find a special friend.

3 = green   4 = blue   5 = brown

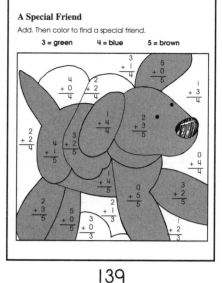

138

139

Add 'Em Up
Add the numbers.

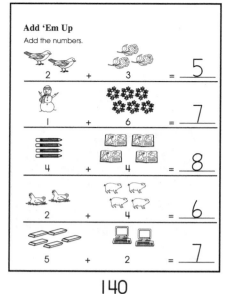

$2 + 3 = 5$

$1 + 6 = 7$

$4 + 4 = 8$

$2 + 4 = 6$

$5 + 2 = 7$

140

Starry Sums
Add the stars in each row. Write the sum on the line.

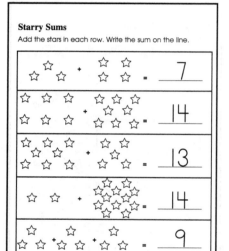

7

14

13

14

9

141

In the Garden

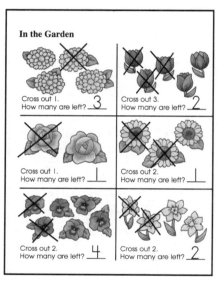

Cross out 1.
How many are left? 3

Cross out 3.
How many are left? 2

Cross out 1.
How many are left? 1

Cross out 2.
How many are left? 1

Cross out 2.
How many are left? 4

Cross out 2.
How many are left? 2

142

How Many Are Left?
Write the numbers that tell how many.

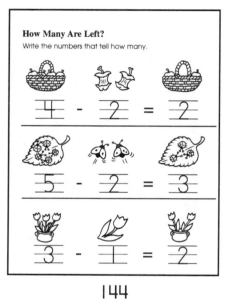

$4 - 2 = 2$

$5 - 2 = 3$

$3 - 1 = 2$

144

Wholes and Halves
Look at the vegetables at the bottom of the page. Draw two halves next to the matching whole vegetable.

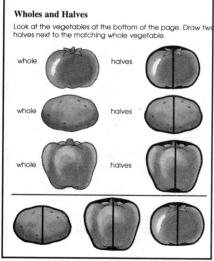

whole   halves

whole   halves

whole   halves

145

Half and Half
Look at the pictures below. Make each object whole by drawing its other half.

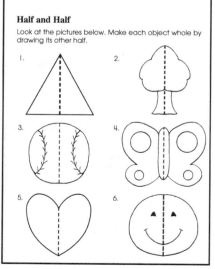

1.   2.

3.   4.

5.   6.

146

Where's the Turtle?

Write the place of the turtle.

first second third fourth fifth

first second __third__ fourth fifth

first second third fourth __fifth__

first __second__ third fourth fifth

147

Friends Go Hiking

The friends are following their leader on the trail.
Draw a line from each number-order word to the matching hiker.

fourth third first second eighth fifth seventh sixth

148

Money Mania

Add the coin values in each row. Write the total amount on the line.

penny 1¢	nickel 5¢	dime 10¢	quarter 25¢	
1.				= 2¢
2.				= 7¢
3.				= 30¢
4.				= 16¢
5.				= 30¢
6.				= 30¢
7.				= 30¢
8.				= 12¢
9.				= 19¢
10.				= 36¢

149

Money Matters

Add the coin values in each row. Write the total amount on the line.

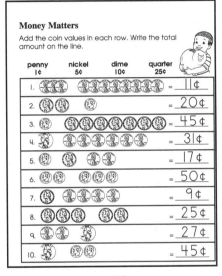

penny 1¢	nickel 5¢	dime 10¢	quarter 25¢	
1.				= 11¢
2.				= 20¢
3.				= 45¢
4.				= 31¢
5.				= 17¢
6.				= 50¢
7.				= 9¢
8.				= 25¢
9.				= 27¢
10.				= 45¢

150

What's Long?

Color the two in each set that are the same length.

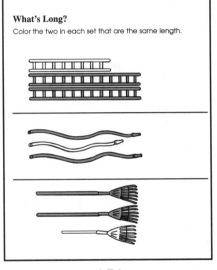

151

Dinosaurs Rule!

Scientists use rulers to measure dinosaur bones.
Write the missing numbers on the rulers.

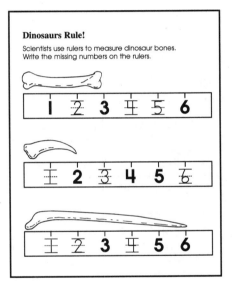

1 2 3 4 5 6

1 2 3 4 5 6

1 2 3 4 5 6

152

I Can Measure

Draw a line from each child to the correct measuring tool.

What does Dan need to measure the sugar?

What does Jen need to weigh the oranges?

What does Jill need to measure how long the ribbon is?

What does Matt need to find out how cold it is?

153

Animal Graphs

Write how many. Circle the animal that has the most. Color the animal that has the least.

3 5 2

154

Funny Frogs

Count the frogs and write the number.
Color a square for each frog.

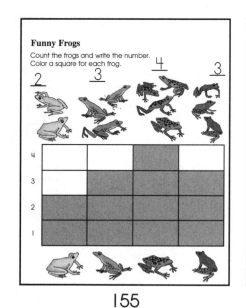

2   3   4   3

4			
3			
2			
1			

155

Days of the Week

Trace the words. Say them.

The first day of the week.

Sunday

The second day of the week.

Monday

The third day of the week.

Tuesday

The fourth day of the week.

Wednesday

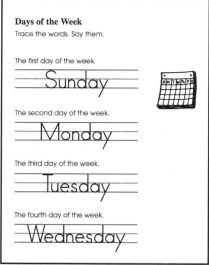

156

More Days of the Week

Trace the words. Say them.

The fifth day of the week.

Thursday

The sixth day of the week.

Friday

The seventh day of the week.

Saturday

What's your favorite day of the week?

Answers will vary.

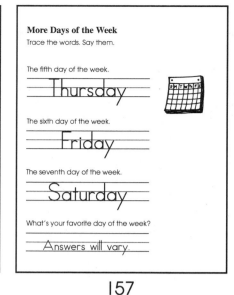

157

Time of Day

Trace and color. Draw a picture of something you do during each time of the day.

morning — Pictures will vary.

afternoon — Pictures will vary.

night — Pictures will vary.

158

Body Parts

Point to the body parts. Say the name of each. Trace the words.

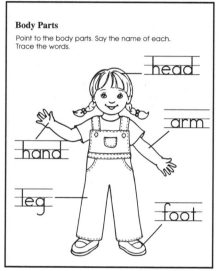

head

arm

hand

leg

foot

159

Left and Right

Draw a ring on the right hand.
Draw a watch on the left wrist.

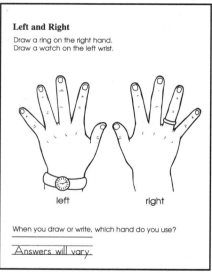

left   right

When you draw or write, which hand do you use?

Answers will vary.

160

My Hair

Draw a picture of your face and hair.

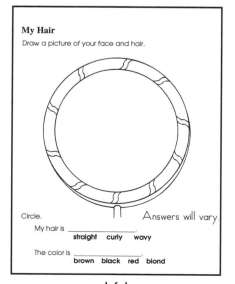

Answers will vary.

Circle.

My hair is _____ straight   curly   wavy

The color is _____ brown   black   red   blond

161

My Feet

Draw a picture of your feet.

Pictures will vary.

Color the things that your feet help you do.

162

My Five Senses

Which parts of the body help you see, hear, smell, taste, and touch? Draw lines to show your answers.

I see with my

I hear with my

I smell with my

I taste with my

I touch with my

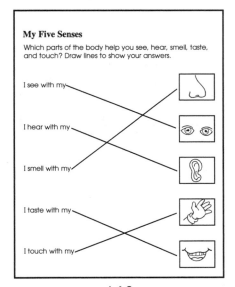

163

My Eyes

Draw a picture of your eyes.

Pictures will vary.

Color the things you like to see. Answers will vary.

164

My Ears

Draw a picture of your ears.

Pictures will vary.

Color the things you like to hear. Answers will vary.

165

My Mouth

Draw a picture of your mouth and teeth.

Pictures will vary.

Color the things you like to eat. Answers will vary.

166

My Hands

Draw a picture of your hands.

Pictures will vary.

Color the things you like to touch. Answers will vary.

167

I Brush My Teeth

Circle the things that you use to brush your teeth.

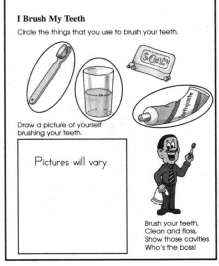

Draw a picture of yourself brushing your teeth.

Pictures will vary.

Brush your teeth,
Clean and floss,
Show those cavities
Who's the boss!

168

I Am Growing

_____ Answers will vary.

I weigh _____ pounds.

I am _____ inches tall.

Color the things that help you grow.

169

I Eat Healthful Snacks

Circle six healthful snacks.

170

Daily Learning Drills Grade K

Let's Eat Dinner!

Read each sentence. Draw a line to the matching picture.

I will eat spaghetti.

I will eat green beans.

I will eat bread.

I will eat a cupcake.

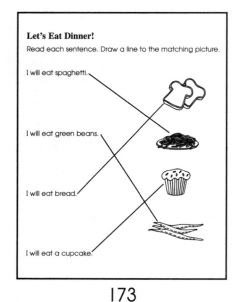

173

My Favorite Food

Finish the sentence. Draw a picture to match.

My favorite dinner meal
is _____ Answers will vary.
My favorite drink is
_____

Here is what I like to eat for dinner.

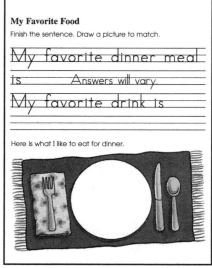

174

Plant at Work

Cut out the pictures. Match and paste them in order.

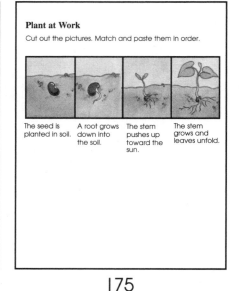

The seed is planted in soil. / A root grows down into the soil. / The stem pushes up toward the sun. / The stem grows and leaves unfold.

175

Plant Fun

Find the word in each row. Color the boxes to show the word.

seed
root
stem
dirt
sun
water
leaf

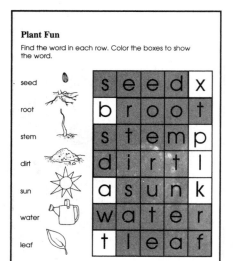

s	e	e	d	x
b	r	o	o	t
s	t	e	m	p
d	i	r	t	l
a	s	u	n	k
w	a	t	e	r
t	l	e	a	f

177

Parts of a Plant

Trace the words and the lines. Color the plant.

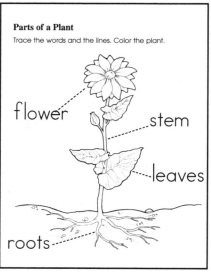

flower
stem
leaves
roots

178

Eating Plants

Trace the words.

We Eat Parts of Plants	corn — We eat seeds.
carrots — We eat roots.	celery — We eat stems.
lettuce — We eat leaves.	apples — We eat fruits.

179

At the Market

Look at the picture. Find **3** foods. Write their names.

oranges / toys / mom / baby / cereal / apples / cart

1. oranges
2. apples
3. cereal

180

Plants We Eat

Circle the words. The words go → and ↓.

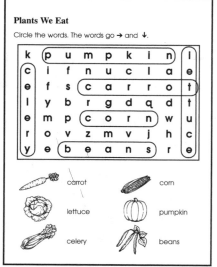

k	p	u	m	p	k	i	n	l
c	i	f	n	u	c	l	a	e
e	f	s	c	a	r	r	o	t
l	y	b	r	g	d	q	d	t
e	m	p	c	o	r	n	w	u
r	o	v	z	m	v	j	h	c
y	e	b	e	a	n	s	r	e

carrot   corn
lettuce   pumpkin
celery   beans

181

Plant Groups

Cross out the plant in each box that does not belong.
Color the other plants.

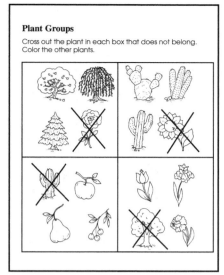

182

Trees Give Many Gifts

Circle the pictures that show ways people use trees and things that come from trees.

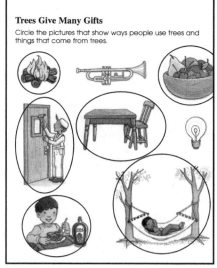

183

A Special Garden

Draw a picture of yourself standing in a garden.

Pictures will vary.

Describe what you see standing in the garden.

I see ___Answers will vary.___
I hear _____
I smell _____
I feel _____

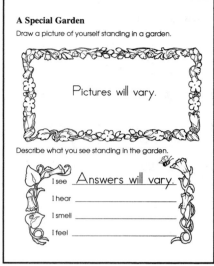

184

Garden Days

Circle and write the best title for each picture.

A Long Nap
No More Weeds
Smell the Flowers

No More Weeds

A Sweet Lunch
A Big Bird
Trees Are Green

A Sweet Lunch

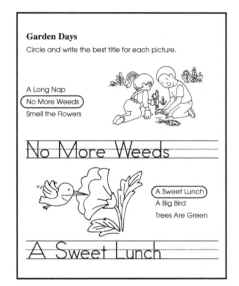

185

Out of Place

Circle 1 thing in each box that does not belong.
Answer the question at the bottom.

Everything circled is a kind of what? ___food___

186

In the Forest

Look at the picture. Find 3 living things.
Write their names.

mountain
trees
bear   fish
rocks   creek

1. ___trees___
2. ___bear___
3. ___fish___

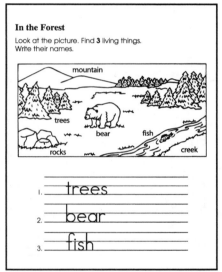

187

At the Farm

Look at the picture. Find 3 living things.
Write their names.

1. ___pigs___
2. ___horse___
3. ___cow___

188

Pets We Like

Color the pictures. Say the words. Check off the pets you have or would like to have.

Answers will vary.

☐ turtle   ☐ bird
☐ snake   ☐ dog
☐ cat   ☐ rabbit

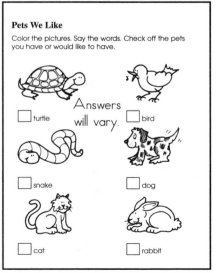

189

How Animals Move

Tell how each animal moves. Trace the words.

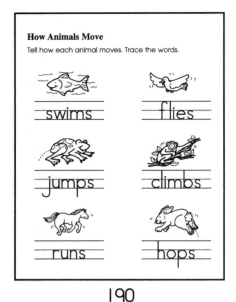

swims   flies

jumps   climbs

runs   hops

190

Flying High

Color the things that fly.

191

I Want My Mommy!

Trace the line from each baby to its mother.

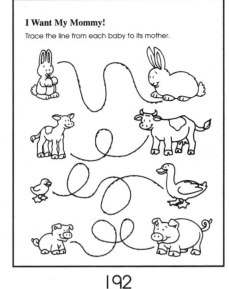

192

Little Lost Lamb

Help the lamb find its mother.

193

Mrs. Cow's Friends

Trace the names of Mrs. Cow's barnyard friends. Color.

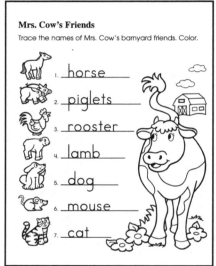

1. horse
2. piglets
3. rooster
4. lamb
5. dog
6. mouse
7. cat

194

Search and Find

Find the objects in the woods. Color them.

deer eggs squirrel fish frog snake

195

A Beaver Family

Help the beavers get out of their house.

196

The Zoo

Finish each sentence with the name of an animal.

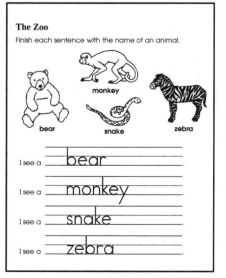

bear   monkey   snake   zebra

I see a bear

I see a monkey

I see a snake

I see a zebra

197

Hear Me Roar!

Connect the dots from 1 to 10. Color.

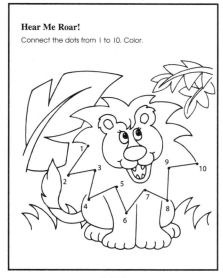

198

Where Are the Tigers?

Help the boy find his way to the tigers.

199

Train Safari

Help the train take the right path through the forest. Watch out for elephants!

201

Rain Forest Animals

Look at the picture. Read the words. Write the words on the lines.

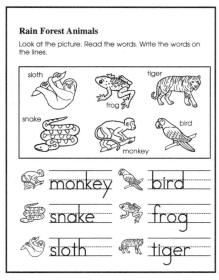

202

What's Wrong?

In each picture, cross out the part that cannot really happen. Color the pictures.

204

Ocean Animals

Write each animal's name in the correct place.

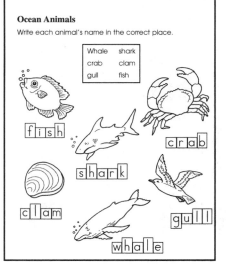

206

Fishy Friends

Help the striped fish swim through the coral and find its friend.

207

Beautiful Birds

Circle the words. The words go → and ↓.

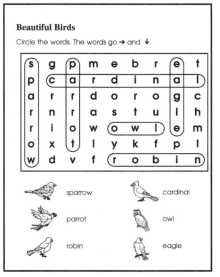

208

Daily Learning Drills Grade K

A Bunch of Butterflies

Color the butterfly that is different.

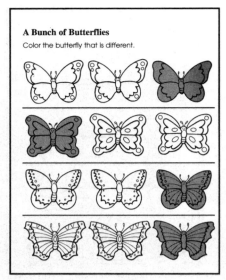

210

Go Buggy!

Unscramble each word. Use the Word Bank for help.
Write the words in the puzzle.

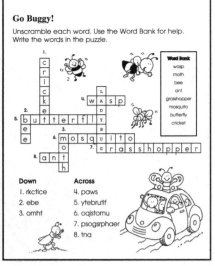

Word Bank
wasp
moth
bee
ant
grasshopper
mosquito
butterfly
cricket

Down
1. rkctice
2. ebe
3. omht

Across
4. paws
5. ytebrutlf
6. oqistomu
7. psogsrphaer
8. tna

211

Bug Walk

Show the bug how to cross the leaf.

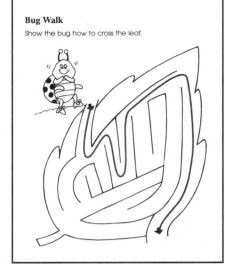

212

A Bunch of Beetles

Find the **3** beetles that match. Color them.

213

Where Is My Home?

Trace each path. Color the pictures.

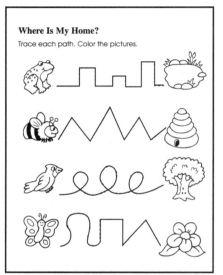

214

Animal Sightings

Cut out each animal card below on the dotted lines. Glue each card under the picture of where you find the animal.

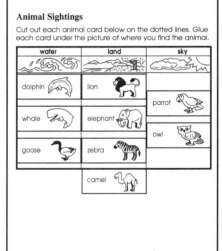

water	land	sky
dolphin	lion	
whale	elephant	parrot
goose	zebra	owl
	camel	

215

A Long Time Ago

Color the scene. Then trace the letters below.

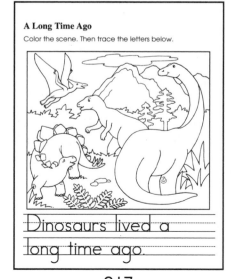

Dinosaurs lived a
long time ago.

217

Maiasaura Maze

Some dinosaurs made nests on the ground. They laid eggs in the nests. Baby dinosaurs hatched from the eggs.

Can you help Mother Maiasaura get back to her nest? Draw a line to show her path. Watch out! T-Rex wants to eat her.

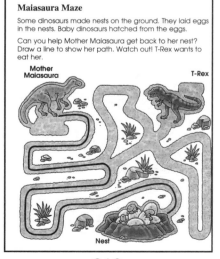

218

Long Gone

Connect the dots from 1 to 25. Color.

219

Plant-Eater or Meat-Eater?

Some dinosaurs ate meat. Some dinosaurs ate plants. Look at the pictures. Circle yes or no to answer the questions.

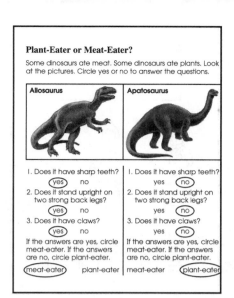

Allosaurus	Apatosaurus

1. Does it have sharp teeth?
(yes)   no

1. Does it have sharp teeth?
yes   (no)

2. Does it stand upright on two strong back legs?
(yes)   no

2. Does it stand upright on two strong back legs?
yes   (no)

3. Does it have claws?
(yes)   no

3. Does it have claws?
yes   (no)

If the answers are yes, circle meat-eater. If the answers are no, circle plant-eater.

(meat-eater)   plant-eater

If the answers are yes, circle meat-eater. If the answers are no, circle plant-eater.

meat-eater   (plant-eater)

220

Seasons

Color the pictures. Trace and say the season words.

winter   spring

summer   fall

221

Spring, Summer, Fall, Winter

Number the events in order. Write a number in each box. Then color the pictures.

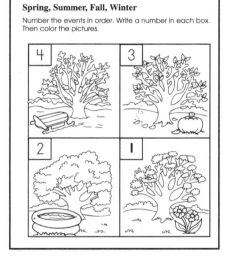

222

Fall Scramble

Unscramble the fall word on each leaf. Color the leaf the correct color.

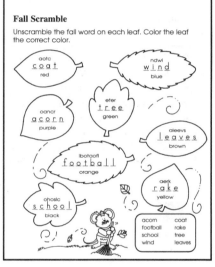

aotc
c o a t
red

ndwi
w i n d
blue

oancr
a c o r n
purple

eter
t r e e
green

aleevs
l e a v e s
brown

ibotaofl
f o o t b a l l
orange

aerk
r a k e
yellow

ohasic
s c h o o l
black

acorn   coat
football   rake
school   tree
wind   leaves

223

Winter Word Search

Circle each winter word from the word box in the puzzle. Check off each word as you find it. Words go across and down.

☐ flakes   ☐ blizzard   ☐ sled   ☐ cold
☐ skate   ☐ snow   ☐ snowman   ☐ freeze
☐ January   ☐ ice   ☐ mittens   ☐ ski

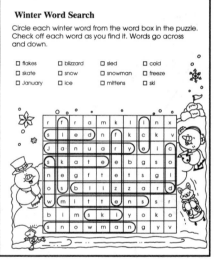

224

How Is the Weather?

Trace and color.

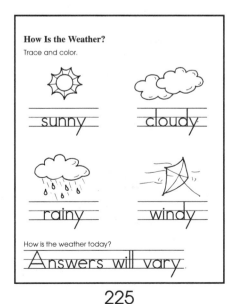

sunny   cloudy

rainy   windy

How is the weather today?

Answers will vary

225

Weather Words

Circle the words. The words go → and ↓.

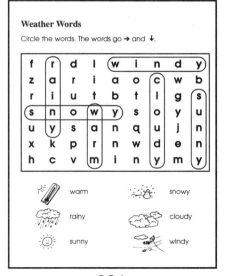

warm   snowy

rainy   cloudy

sunny   windy

226

Cold or Warm?

Look at the clothes each child is wearing.
Circle **cold** if the child is dressed for cold weather.
Circle **warm** if the child is dressed for warm weather.

227

How Does It Feel Outside?

Write a word for each picture.

| hot | warm | cold |

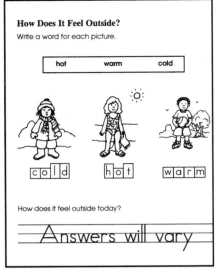

c o l d   h o t   w a r m

How does it feel outside today?

Answers will vary

228

Rain or Shine

Look at each weather forecast on the left and draw a line
to show what the girl should wear.

229

Off to Space!

Connect the dots from **1** to **25**. Color to finish the picture.

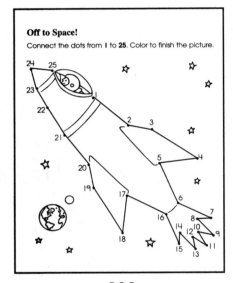

230

Far Out!

Circle the words. The words go → and ↓.

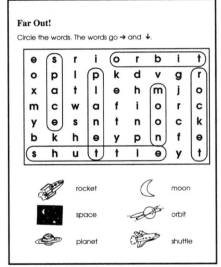

rocket   moon
space   orbit
planet   shuttle

231

My Name

Write your name.

First name

Answers will vary

Middle name

Last name

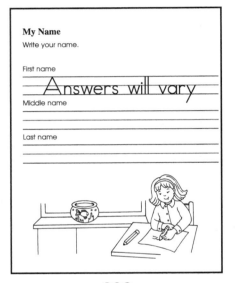

232

Baby Days

Draw a picture of yourself when you were a baby.

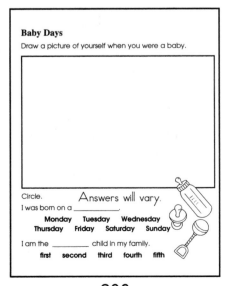

Circle.   Answers will vary.
I was born on a _____.
Monday   Tuesday   Wednesday
Thursday   Friday   Saturday   Sunday

I am the _____ child in my family.
first   second   third   fourth   fifth

233

Happy Birthday

Draw candles to show how old you are.

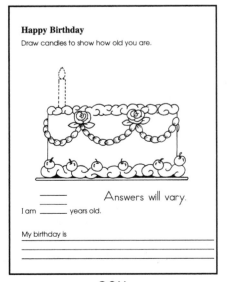

_____   Answers will vary.
I am _____ years old.

My birthday is _____

234

Look What I Can Do!

Put a ✓ in the box if you do the activity each day.

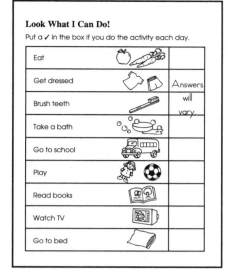

Eat		Answers will vary.
Get dressed		
Brush teeth		
Take a bath		
Go to school		
Play		
Read books		
Watch TV		
Go to bed		

235

Getting Bigger Each Day

Color the things that you can do now. Circle the things that you want to learn to do. Continue on the next page.

Answers will vary.

236

Answers will vary.

237

My Favorite Toy

Draw a picture of your favorite toy.

Answers will vary.

Color other toys you like.

239

My Family Laughs!

Draw a picture showing something that makes your family laugh.

Pictures will vary.

Color the things that make you laugh.

Answers will vary.

240

I Can Get Mad

Color the pictures that make you feel mad.

241

I Get Scared

Answers will vary.

Color the pictures of things that scare you.

242

My Family

Trace the words. Draw a picture of your family.

father sister mother
grandmother
brother grandfather

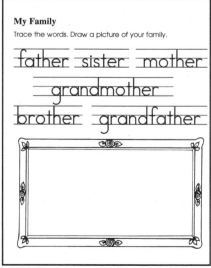

243

Daily Learning Drills Grade K

We Do Things Together

Look at each picture. If your family likes to do what is shown, color the picture.

Answers will vary.

244

Answers will vary.

245

My Jobs

Answers will vary.

Color the pictures of the jobs you do.

246

When I Am Older

Answers will vary.

Color the pictures of the jobs that you would like to do someday.

247

I Play Inside

Color the things you could play with inside.
Draw an X on the things you could not play with inside.

248

Indoor and Outdoor Fun

Color the things you use inside yellow. Color the things you use outside blue.

outside   inside   outside

outside   inside   outside

outside   inside   inside

249

My Friends

Draw a picture of two of your friends.

My friends' names are ___ Answers will vary

and ___

We like to ___

250

Friends Are Polite

Look at each picture.
Write the polite sentences next to the matching pictures.

Say this if you ask for something.   Please.

Say this if your friend gives you something.   Thank you!

Say this if you hurt your friend's feelings.   I'm sorry.

251

Friends Have Fun

Draw a line to the picture that completes the sentence.

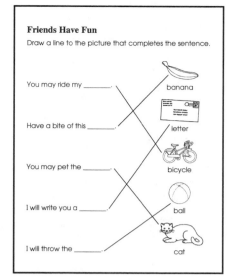

You may ride my _____.

Have a bite of this _____.

You may pet the _____.

I will write you a _____.

I will throw the _____.

banana

letter

bicycle

ball

cat

252

Chef Charlie

Chef Charlie tossed the pizza crust. Where did it go?

253

When I Grow Up

Color the pictures that show what you might be when you grow up.

Answers will vary.

A B C

254

When I grow up, I want to be a

_____

Answers will vary

255

Learning the Past

Help the museum guide find the dinosaur display.

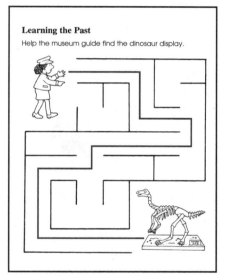

256

To the Rescue

Connect the dots from **A** to **Z**. Color.

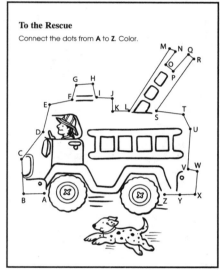

257

Places

Draw lines to show where each item belongs.
Say the names of the places.

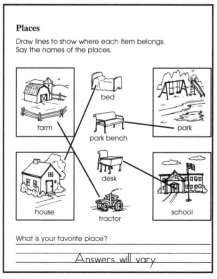

farm

bed

park bench

park

house

desk

tractor

school

What is your favorite place?

_____

Answers will vary

258

A Busy Day

Circle the things that are in the picture.

259

Daily Learning Drills Grade K

Off to School

Connect the dots from **A** to **Z**.

260

A Classroom

Finish each sentence with the name of what you see.

You will go to the table .

You will go to the rug .

You will go to the books .

You will go to the fish .

261

School Time

Color the pictures. Check off the boxes of the things you do at school.

☐ sing   Answers will vary.   ☐ draw

☐ count   ☐ paint

☐ read   ☐ write

262

Playground Fun

Trace the words.

swing   climb

slide   kick

What do you like to do at the playground?

Answers will vary.

263

Safety Sign Match

Draw a line from each safety sign to its shadow.

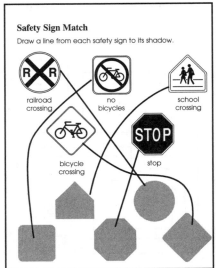

railroad crossing   no bicycles   school crossing

bicycle crossing   stop

264

Workers Use Transportation

Draw lines to match the pictures.

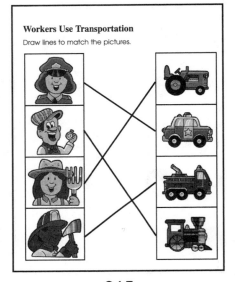

265

Words to Know

Look at the picture. Read the words. Write the words on the lines.

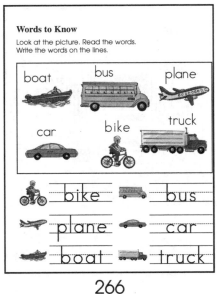

boat   bus   plane

car   bike   truck

bike   bus

plane   car

boat   truck

266

A Busy Street

Look at the picture. Write **3** things that people ride.

tree   bike   car   house

truck

mailbox

1. bike

2. car

3. truck

267

Let's Go!

Color the spaces with words for ways to travel.

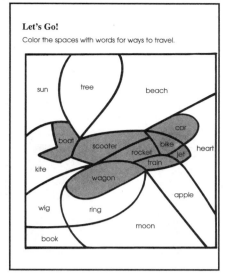

268

Look and Find

Find three kinds of transportation.
Trace each one with a different color.

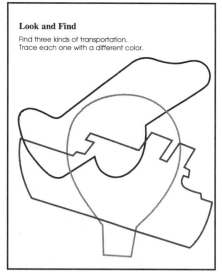

269

On the Go!

Draw a line from each picture to the word that describes
what it travels on. Then color the pictures.

| air | water | land |

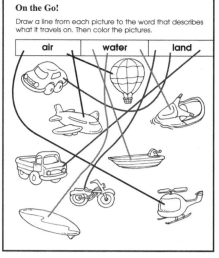

270

Getting There

Check off each kind of transportation you have used.
Draw a circle around a kind of transportation you
would like to try some day. Answers will vary.

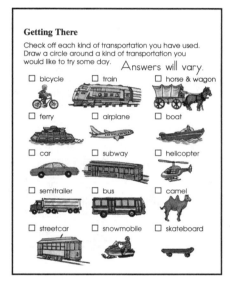

□ bicycle   □ train   □ horse & wagon

□ ferry   □ airplane   □ boat

□ car   □ subway   □ helicopter

□ semitrailer   □ bus   □ camel

□ streetcar   □ snowmobile   □ skateboard

271

Going on a Trip

Where would you like to go on a trip? Draw it.
Trace and finish the sentence.

I will go to

Answers will vary.

272

Answers will vary.

Color the things that you will take on your trip.

273

Away We Go

Circle and write the best title for each picture.

The Big Plane
Trains Are Fun
(Going to Camp)

Going to Camp

A Snowy Day
(On Our Boat)
At the Zoo

On Our Boat

274

If I Could Go Anywhere . . .

Draw a picture to show where you would like to visit.

I would like to visit

Answers will vary.

275

Daily Learning Drills Grade K

Halloween Puzzle

Read each clue. Write the correct word in the puzzle space

Down
1. You wear me.
3. I taste good on apples.
4. I spin my own home.

Across
1. I am made of apples.
2. What you say on Halloween
   is "_____-or-treat"
5. I grow on a tree.
6. You get me on Halloween.

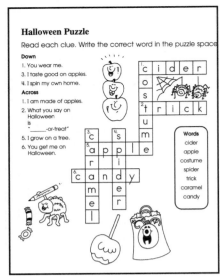

Words
cider
apple
costume
spider
trick
caramel
candy

276

Search for Spring Holiday Words

Circle each spring word in the word search.
Check off each word on the list as you find it in the puzzle.
Words go across and down.

☐ bunny
☐ tree
☐ chocolate
☐ bonnet
☐ carrot
☐ hop
☐ rain
☐ egg
☐ grass
☐ grow
☐ flower
☐ rabbit
☐ chick
☐ basket
☐ candy
☐ sun

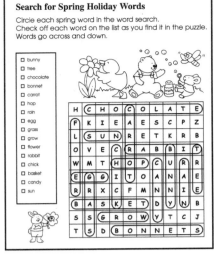

279

Don't Litter

Color the picture of the seashore. Then put a big **X** on all the trash that should go in the trash can. There are five pieces of trash.

282

City or Village Life

Color the pictures that show city life **blue**. Color the pictures that show village live **orange**. Color the pictures that can be village or city live **red**.

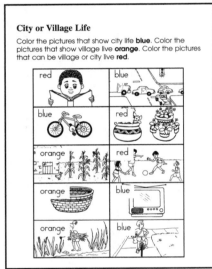

283

Mountain Maze

One of Maria's chores is collecting reeds for weaving baskets. Help Maria find her way through the mountain trails to get to the river bank where the reeds grow.

284

The Great Wall

The longest structure in the world is in China. It is called the Great Wall. Work your way through the Great Wall maze.

285

Chinese Calendar

When is your birthday? _Answers will vary._

In which Chinese year were you born? _____

What is the animal sign for your Chinese birth year? _____

Color the animals in the calendar.

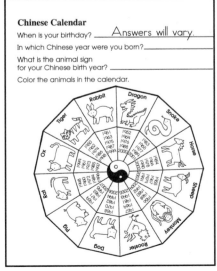

286

Map Activity

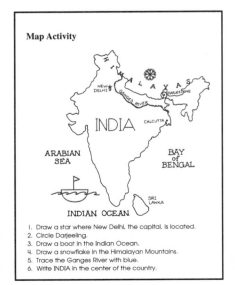

1. Draw a star where New Delhi, the capital, is located.
2. Circle Darjeeling.
3. Draw a boat in the Indian Ocean.
4. Draw a snowflake in the Himalayan Mountains.
5. Trace the Ganges River with blue.
6. Write INDIA in the center of the country.

287

Name _____

Fishing Fun

Find the letters from **A** to **M**. Color them.

A   B   C   D   E   F   G   H   I   J   K   L

Name _____

Shining Bright

To find the mystery letter, color the spaces with the following letters red.

Q F V P G O M N U

Q	G	M	N
S	A	J	W
U	F	P	H
O	L	T	Z
V	Y	R	B

Circle the mystery letter.   **E   F   P**

Name _____

The Alphabet Patch

Trace the letters.

Name _____

I Can Write the ABC's

Trace the letters.

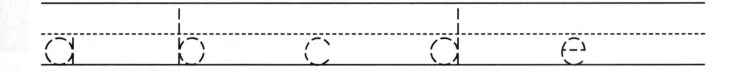

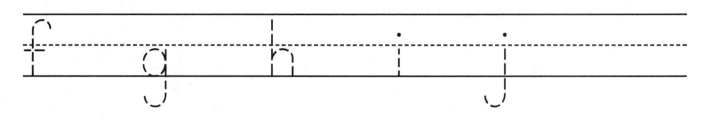

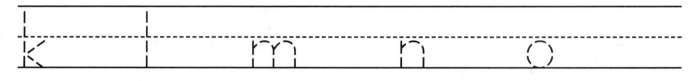

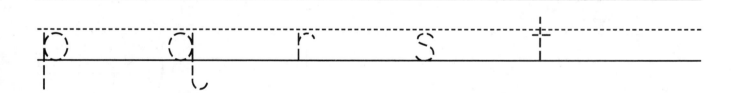

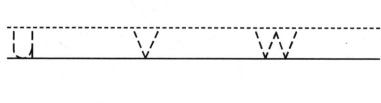

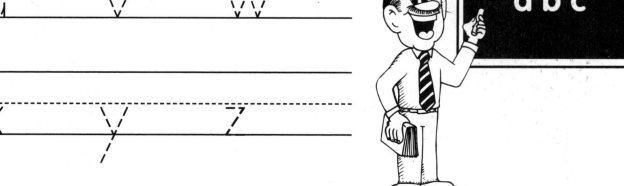

Name _____

Haystack Match

Draw a line from the capital letter to its lowercase letter.

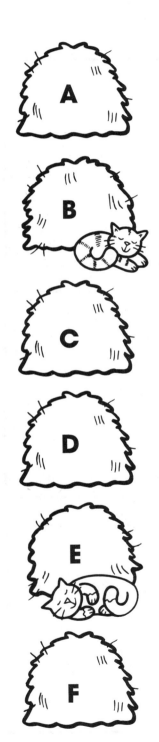

Daily Learning Drills Grade K

Name _____

Nifty New Words

Write the first letter for each picture.
Read the new word. Draw a picture of it in the box.

1.

___   ___   ___

2.

___   ___   ___

3.

___   ___   ___

Name _____

Picnic

Find these things, which begin with **c**. Color them yellow.
Then color the rest of the picture.

cat	can	cap	cloud	cake

Daily Learning Drills Grade K

Name _____

Grandma's Goodies

Find these things, which begin with **p**. Color them purple.
Then color the rest of the picture.

pie   pencil   pen   pig   peanut

Name _____

Puzzling Words

Fill in the blanks with **s, sl, sm, sn,** or **st.**
Write the words in the puzzle.

1.  ___ ___ed

2. ___ ___amp

3.  ___ ___ow

4. ___ ___ide

5. ___eal

6. ___ ___ile

7. ___ ___ail

Daily Learning Drills Grade K

Name _____

Same Sounds

Look at each box. Say the name of the picture on the left.
Draw lines from it to the pictures that have the same
beginning sound.

Animal Races

Look at the animals in each row. Circle the animal moving in a different direction.

Name _____

Be a Dinosaur Detective

Look at the picture below. Can you find **5** mistakes?
Color them.

Name _____

Opposites

Trace the words. Draw lines between the opposites.

hot

in

old

over

under

new

out

cold

Name _____

I Play Outside

In each box, circle the group of words that matches the words at the top of the box.

in the sand

in the sand

in the send

on a swing

on a swing

on a string

behind a tree

behind a tray

behind a tree

by a pond

by a pond

by a pane

Name _____

What Happens Next?

Look at the pictures. Write the sentences.

Will she go in the pool?

_____

1. _____ ?

She will go in the pool.

_____

2. _____ .

LANGUAGE ARTS REVIEW

Humpty Dumpty

Write the words where they belong.

a   sat   had   the   fall   and   put   men

_____   _____

Humpty Dumpty _____ on _____ wall.

_____   _____

Humpty Dumpty _____ a great _____.

_____   _____

All _____ king's horses _____ all the

_____   _____

king's _____ couldn't _____

Humpty together again.

Name _____

Over or Under

Look at the pictures. Tell whether the object is **over** or **under** the tree. Trace and color.

over

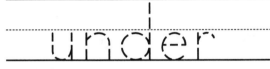

under

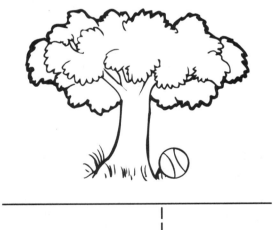

under

over

Name _____

Colors

Circle the words. The words go → and ↓ .

p	i	f	d	k	b	l	u	e
u	g	m	r	b	r	e	g	p
r	y	e	l	l	o	w	r	b
p	i	n	k	a	w	h	e	l
l	o	r	e	d	n	i	e	a
e	p	e	l	s	m	t	n	c
c	o	r	a	n	g	e	w	k

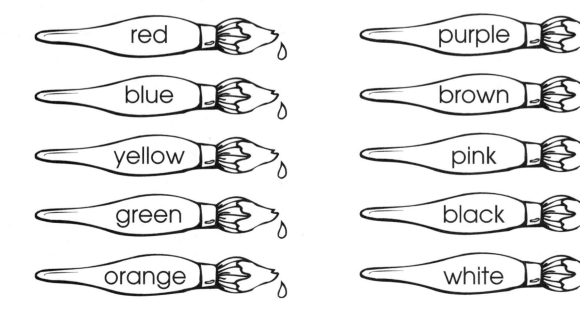

red

blue

yellow

green

orange

purple

brown

pink

black

white

Name _____

Find the Rhyming Words

Look at each row. Circle the picture that rhymes with the first picture in the row.

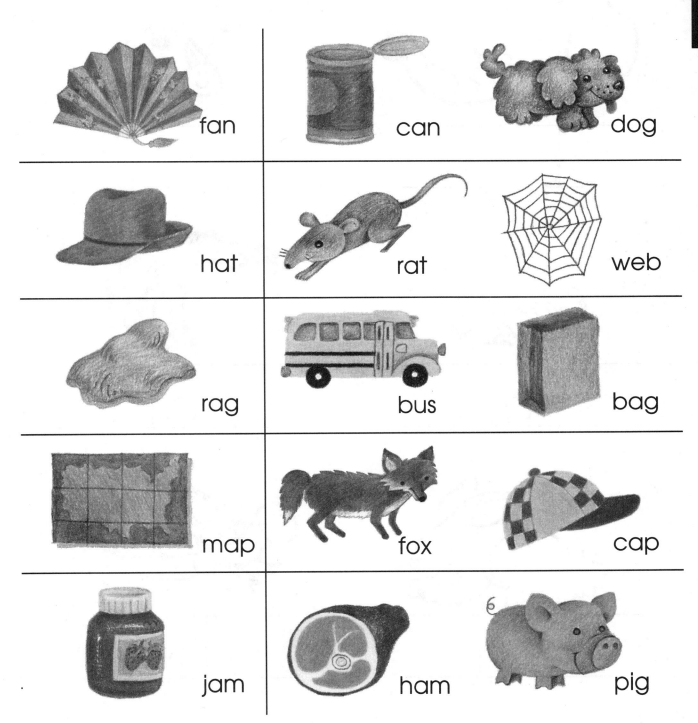

fan   can   dog

hat   rat   web

rag   bus   bag

map   fox   cap

jam   ham   pig

Daily Learning Drills Grade K

Name _____

Size Words

Trace and color.

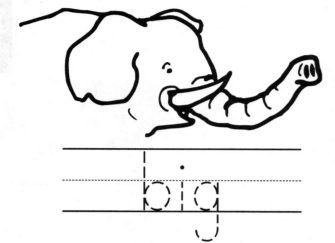

big

small

short

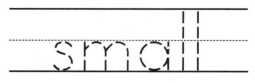

tall

fast

slow

Name _____

Who Needs This?

Look at the first picture in each row.
Color the picture that shows who needs it.

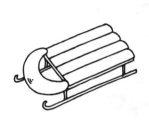  

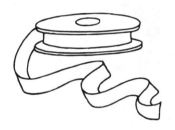  

Small, Medium, Large

Look at the **small**, **medium**, and **large** doghouses.
Draw lines to match the dog to the doghouse.

Name _____

Faces at the Zoo

Circle the animal that comes next in each row.

Name _____

Pass the Ketchup

Color the triangles to lead the boy to the ketchup.

Name _____

Square Surprises

Count the squares. Color them.

Circle to show how many squares you found.

1 **2** **3** **4** **5** **6** **7** **8** **9**

10

Name _____

Color by Number

Color the shapes below according to the color-by-number chart. You will see something that is fun to play with in the spring.

1 – yellow   **2 – white**   **3 – blue**   **4 – green**

5 – orange   **6 – red**   **7 – black**   **8 – purple**

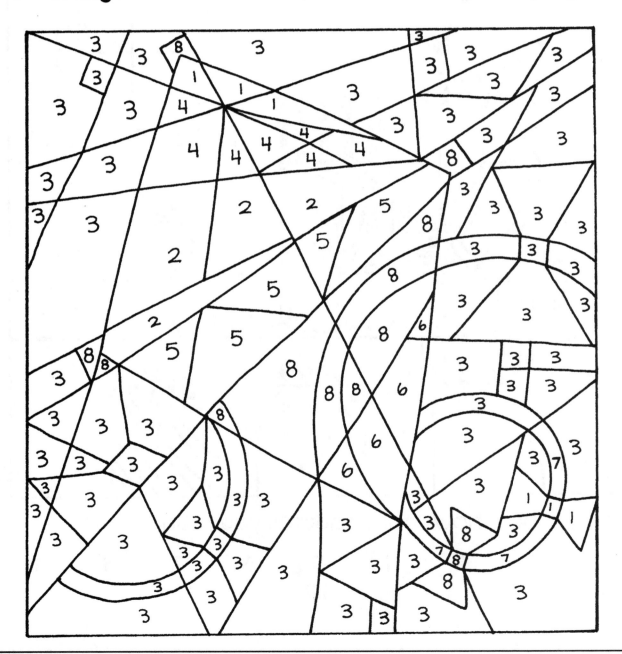

Name _____

Happy Hippo

Write the missing numbers.
Color.

1	___	3	___	5
6	7	___	___	___
1 1	___	13	___	___
___	17	___	___	___

Daily Learning Drills Grade K

Name _____

Lining Them Up

Unscramble and write the number words.

1. nnei ___ ___ ___ ___

2. neves ___ ___ ___ ___ ___

3. wetlev ___ ___ ___ ___ ___ ___

4. etreh ___ ___ ___ ___ ___

5. xis ___ ___ ___

6. etn ___ ___ ___

7. neo ___ ___ ___

8. efvi ___ ___ ___ ___

9. eeenlv ___ ___ ___ ___ ___ ___

10. wot ___ ___ ___

11. theig ___ ___ ___ ___ ___

12. rufo ___ ___ ___ ___

one
two
three
four
five
six
seven
eight
nine
ten
eleven
twelve

Name _____

A Good Harvest

Connect the dots from **1** to **20.** Color.

Name _____

Fall Hunt

Color the hidden pictures. Count each group and write
the number in the correct box.

Name _____

Barnyard Buddies

Find the hidden numbers **1** to **17**. Color them.
Color the rest of the picture.

MATH REVIEW

Name _____

Nature Run

Color **5** flowers.

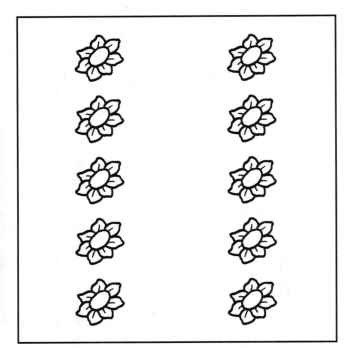

Color **7** suns.

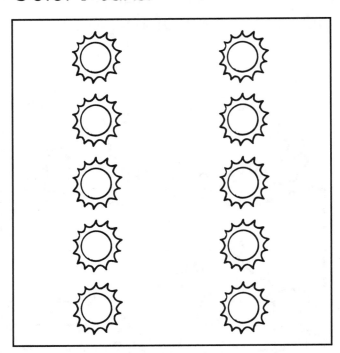

Color **4** trees.

Color **6** birds.

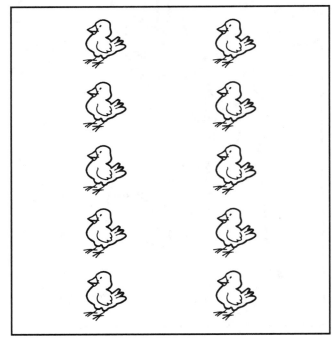

Name _____

Count the Monkeys

Count the monkeys in each box.
Write the number on the line.

_____

_____

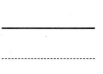

_____

_____

Daily Learning Drills Grade K

MATH REVIEW

Name _____

Batter Up!

Find the baseballs . Color them red. Then color the rest of the picture. Can you find **13** baseballs in all?

354

Name _____

Go Fish!

There are fifteen hidden fish in this picture. Draw a circle around each fish as you find it.

Daily Learning Drills Grade K

Name _____

Sea Friends

Color the picture. Count the sea animals.
Answer the question below.

How many sea animals are there? _____

Name _____

Hungry Baby Bunnies

Help Betsy Bunny find the carrots for her babies. Color the path that goes in order from **1** to **10**.

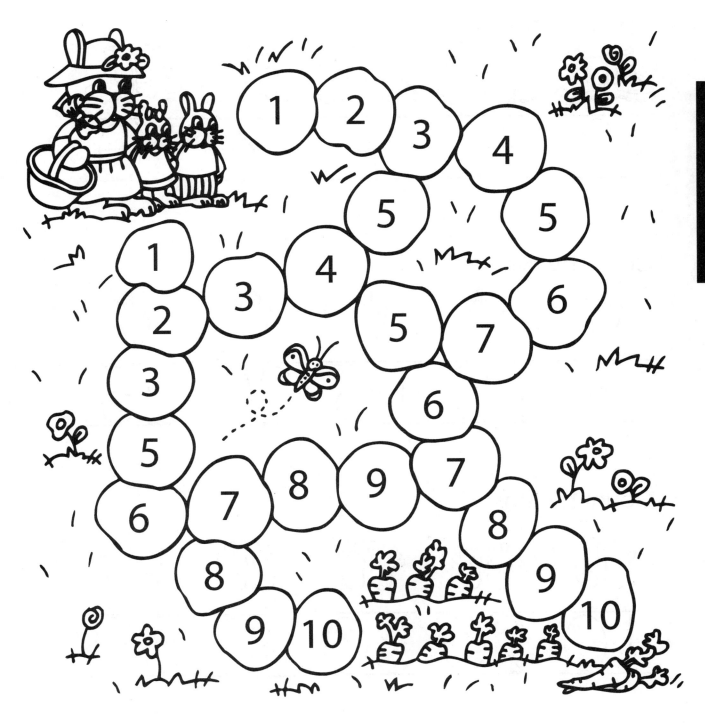

Name _____

Skip Counting

Trace the numbers.

Count by twos.

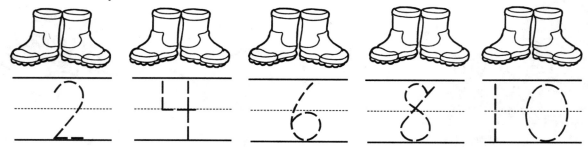

2 4 6 8 10

Count by fives.

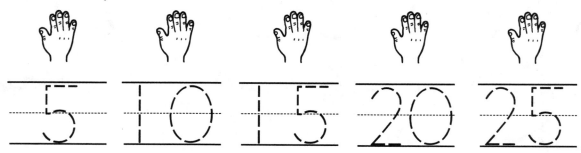

5 10 15 20 25

Count by tens.

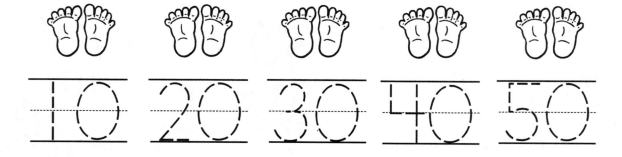

10 20 30 40 50

Name _____

Monkeys Love Bananas!

Solve each problem. Write the answer on the line.

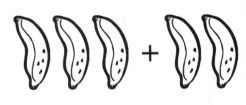

2 + 1 =___

1 + 3 =___

1 + 1 = ___

3 + 2 =___

4 + 1 = ___

1 + 0 =___

Name _____

Away They Go

Cross out. Write how many are left.

$5 - 3 =$ 2

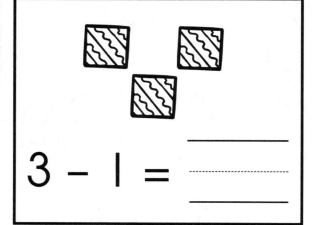

$3 - 1 =$ _____

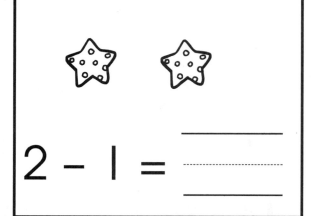

$2 - 1 =$ _____

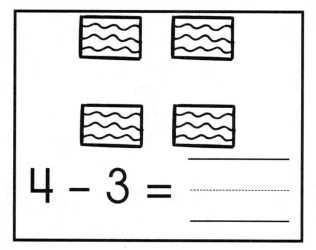

$4 - 3 =$ _____

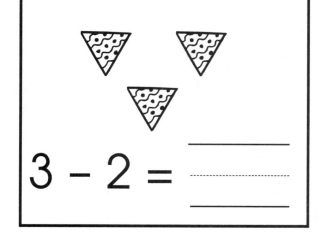

$3 - 2 =$ _____

Name _____

What's the Order?

first   **second**   **third**   **fourth**   **fifth**

In what order are the people lined up?
Draw lines to match.

The is _____.   first

The is _____.   second

The is _____.   third

The is _____.   fourth

The is _____.   fifth

Name _____

Do They Measure Up?

Use a ruler to measure the objects below.

1. _____ inch

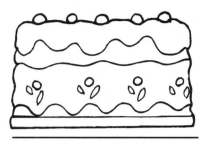

2. _____ inches

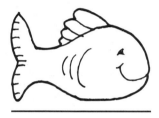

3. _____ inches

4. _____ inches

5. _____ inches

6. _____ inches

7. _____ inches

8. _____ inch

Name _____

Body Count

Count your body parts. Cut out the body-part cards to match the number your body has. Glue under the correct numeral.

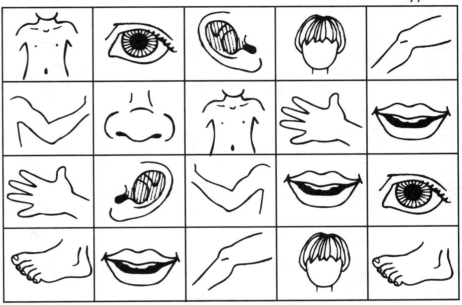

1	2

SCIENCE REVIEW

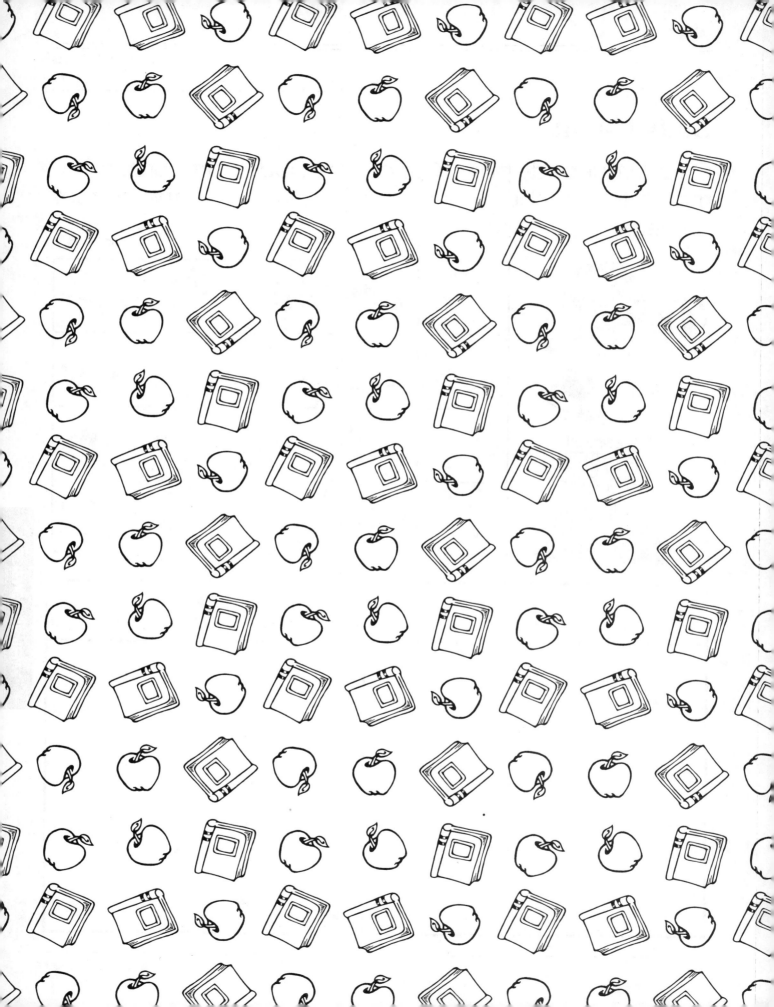

Name _____

I Use My Senses

Draw pictures to show what you like to see, hear, smell, taste, and touch.

see	hear
smell	taste
touch	

Name _____

I Take Care of My Body

Does the picture show a way to take care of your body?
Circle **yes** or **no**.

yes   no

yes   no

yes   no

yes   no

yes   no

yes   no

Name _____

Delicious Food

Color the pictures. Say the words.
Check off the food you like to eat.

☐ apple

☐ corn

☐ egg

☐ beans

☐ bread

☐ cheese

☐ peach

☐ orange

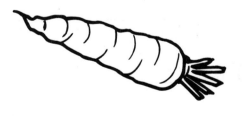

☐ carrot

SCIENCE REVIEW

Daily Learning Drills Grade K

Name _____

I Like Fruit!

Finish each sentence with the name of a fruit.

bananas

apples

grapes

pears

I like _____.

I like _____.

I like _____.

I like _____.

Name _____

Plant Part Game

Color and cut out. Put the parts together to make a plant. Next put them together differently to make a "crazy" plant.

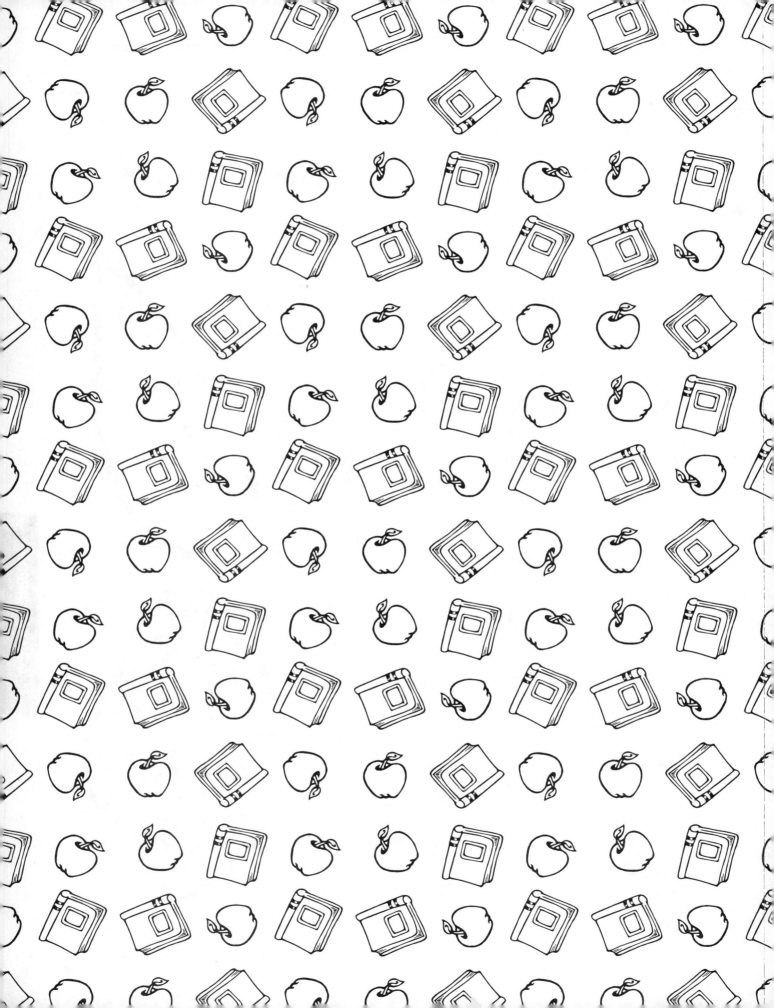

Name _____

My Favorite Kind of Plant

Color the picture. Then complete the sentences.

My favorite kind of plant is a

_____

- -

_____

I like it because

_____

- -

_____

Name _____

Living or Not?

Color the pictures of living things.

pony 	pig 	ball 
doll 	lamb 	snowman 
rain 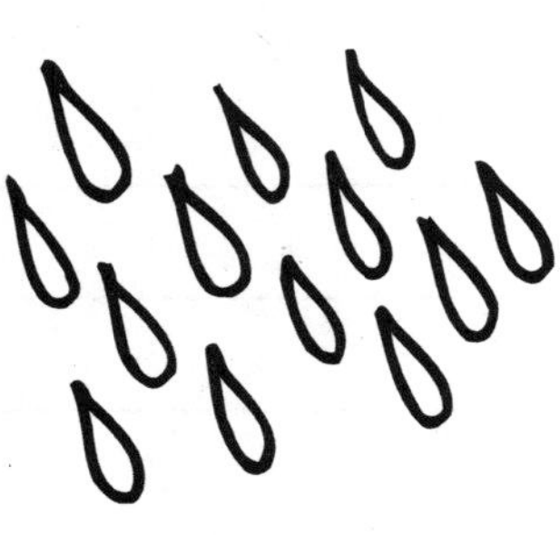	chicken 	duck 

Name _____

At the Beach

Look at the picture. Find **3** living things.
Write their names.

_____

1. _____

_____

2. _____

_____

3. _____

Daily Learning Drills Grade K

SCIENCE REVIEW

Name _____

Mother's Love

Draw a line from each baby animal to its mother.

Name _____

Shadow Match

Say the name of each animal and color. Draw
a line to match each animal with its shadow.

cow

chicken

pig

horse

SCIENCE REVIEW

Name _____

Going to the Zoo

Circle the words. The words go ➡ and ⬇ .

k	d	y	t	l	c	i	k	b
m	j	g	i	r	a	f	f	e
o	s	p	g	f	f	l	r	a
n	t	o	e	v	e	i	o	r
k	b	g	r	y	d	o	h	h
e	l	e	p	h	a	n	t	z
y	r	a	u	x	r	w	m	c

 elephant

 tiger

 giraffe

 lion

 monkey

 bear

Name _____

In the Rain Forest

Circle the plants and animals that are in the picture.

Name _____

Parts of a Crab

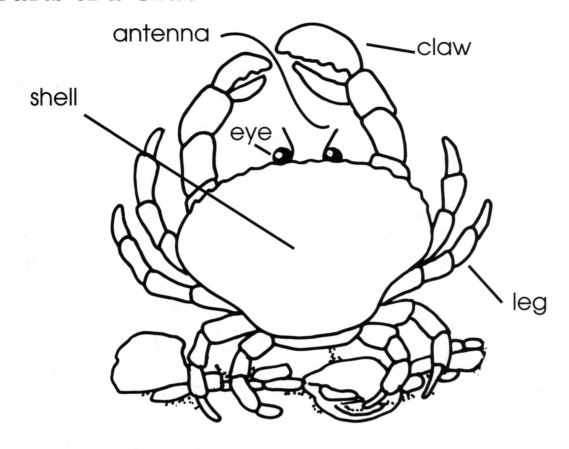

Is it part of a crab? circle **yes** or **no**.

shell	**yes**	**no**	leg	**yes**	**no**
tail	**yes**	**no**	claw	**yes**	**no**
eye	**yes**	**no**	antenna	**yes**	**no**

Name _____

Going Home

Draw a line to help each animal find its home.

SCIENCE REVIEW

Name _____

Animals, Animals Everywhere

Color the animals. Cut out the pictures.
Paste them where they belong.

 Air	 Water	 Ground

Name _____

Dino Pet!

If you could have a pet dinosaur, what would it look like?
Draw your dinosaur below. Write its name on the line.

_____

- -

_____

Name _____

Looking at the Seasons

Cross out the things that do not belong with each season.

spring

fall

summer

winter

Name _____

I Am Special

Draw a picture of yourself. Write your name.

My name is

_____

- -

_____

- -

_____

Name _____

I Can Use These Things

Color the objects you can use.

Name _____

Things I Like

Look at each picture. Say the word.
Is it something you like? Check **yes** or **no**.

gift

yes ☐   no ☐

milk

yes ☐   no ☐

dog

yes ☐   no ☐

books

yes ☐   no ☐

SOCIAL STUDIES REVIEW

Name _____

My Favorite Things

Color the pictures of things you like.

Name _____

A Book About Me

Color this page with drawings. Cut out the book and fold on the dotted lines.

Daily Learning Drills Grade K

Name _____

Follow the directions to make drawings about you.

This is what I do best.

This is one of my favorite things.

Here is someone with whom
I like to play.

Here is what I want to be some day.

Name _____

Feelings

Trace. Draw the child's face to match the feeling.

happy

sad

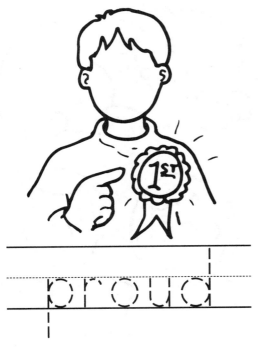

proud

angry

SOCIAL STUDIES REVIEW

Name _____

I Am Happy

Color the pictures that make you feel happy.

Name _____

My Fantastic Family

_____

How many people are in your family? _____

Write their names.

_____

_____

_____

_____

Draw a picture of your family.

Name _____

Family Fun

Draw a picture of a family having fun inside the house.
Draw a picture of a family having fun outside.

Name _____

Time for Chores

Read the rhyme. Then look at the pictures.
Circle the chores you help out with.

> Jack and Jill went up the hill
> To fetch a pail of water.
> Jack fell down, and broke his crown,
> And Jill came tumbling after.

wash dishes

wash the car

take out trash

set the table

iron clothes

make the bed

cook meals

put away toys

cut the grass

Name _____

Toys

Color the pictures. Say the names of the toys.
Circle the toys you like to play with.

truck   blocks   ball

drum   doll   bat

pail   top   balloon

Name _____

Who Helps You?

Circle the words. The words go → and ↓ .

b	t	k	t	w	i	r	d	o
p	a	r	e	n	t	s	e	f
z	n	p	a	r	d	l	n	f
r	d	o	c	t	o	r	t	i
h	y	f	h	e	c	o	i	c
s	p	f	e	n	u	r	s	e
v	n	i	r	u	w	j	t	r

 parents

 nurse

 teacher

 dentist

 doctor

 officer

Daily Learning Drills Grade K

SOCIAL STUDIES REVIEW

Name _____

A Milking Maze

Can you help the farmers get to their cows? Read each clue.
Draw a path that goes by the dairy food named to the cow.
Use a new color for each path.

Name _____

Places to Go

Look at each picture clue. Look in the Word Box for the place you would find that thing.
Write the word in the puzzle.

Word Box

market

bakery

bank

library

park

movies

Down ↓

1.

3.

Across →

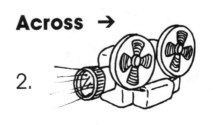

2.

3.

4.

5.

Daily Learning Drills Grade K

Name _____

What a Great Place!

Fill in the puzzle with words that name the pictures below.
Use the Word Box to help you.

1.
2.
3.
4.
5.
6.

Word Box
teacher
pencil
book
crayons
eraser
chalk

1.

2.

3.

4.

5.

6.

The letters in the circles going down spell a
mystery word. The word names a place where all
these things can be found.

Write the word. _____

Name _____

Teacher's Helper

Lead the teacher to her chalkboard.

Daily Learning Drills Grade K

SOCIAL STUDIES REVIEW

Name _____

School Supplies

Color the pictures. Write the word for each picture.

pencil   **glue**   **scissors**   **crayon**

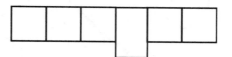

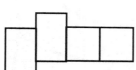

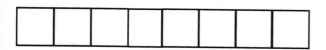

Name _____

Reading Signs

Read each sign. Draw a line to the matching picture.

Daily Learning Drills Grade K

SOCIAL STUDIES REVIEW

Name _____

Ways to Travel

Write a word for each picture.

boat   **plane**   **car**   **train**

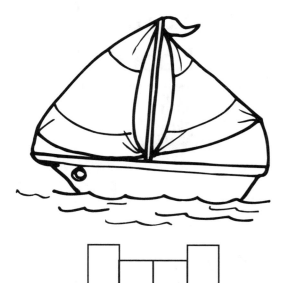

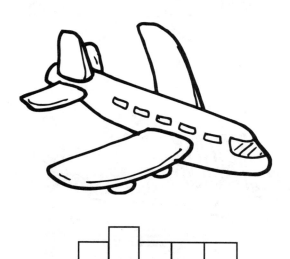

Name _____

Go For a Car Ride!

Choose the correct word below to complete each sentence. Write each word in the correct puzzle square. Then read the black boxes from top to bottom to find another travel word!

Word Bank

luggage   postcard

gift   beach

hotel   home

travel   plane

camera   map

1. Don't forget to take lots of pictures with the _____.

2. Will all the _____ fit in the trunk of our car?

3. Each summer we _____ to a different state.

4. Please mail a _____ to me while you are away.

5. Can you find this highway on the _____?

6. We stayed overnight at a _____.

7. Let's go swimming at the _____.

8. I bought a _____ for my friend Sue.

9. Our _____ landed at the airport on time.

10. It is always good to come back _____ again.

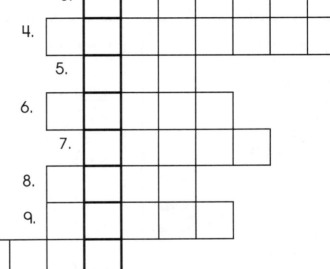

Daily Learning Drills Grade K

SOCIAL STUDIES REVIEW

Review Answer Key

Fishing Fun

Find the letters from **A** to **M**. Color them.

A B C D E F G H I J K L M

321

Shining Bright

To find the mystery letter, color the spaces with the following letters red.

Q F V P G O M N U S

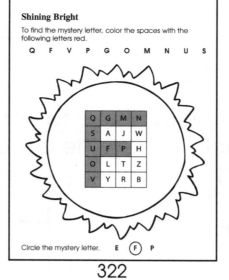

Circle the mystery letter.　　E (F) P

322

The Alphabet Patch

Trace the letters.

323

I Can Write the ABC's

Trace the letters.

324

Haystack Match

Draw a line from the capital letter to its lowercase letter.

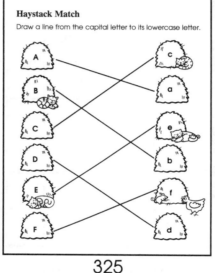

325

Nifty New Words

Write the first letter for each picture.
Read the new word. Draw a picture of it in the box.

1.
m a p　　Pictures will vary.

2.
n e t

3.
c a t

326

Picnic

Find these things, which begin with **c**. Color them yellow.
Then color the rest of the picture.

cat　can　cap　cloud　cake

327

Grandma's Goodies

Find these things, which begin with **p**. Color them purple.
Then color the rest of the picture.

pie　pencil　pen　pig　peanut

328

Puzzling Words

Fill in the blanks with **s, sl, sm, sn,** or **st**.
Write the words in the puzzle.

1. s l ed
2. s t amp
3. s n ow
4. s l ide
5. s eal
6. s m ile
7. s n ail

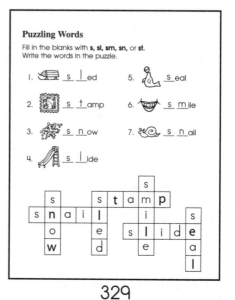

329

Same Sounds

Look at each box. Say the name of the picture on the left. Draw lines from it to the pictures that have the same beginning sound.

Animal Races

Look at the animals in each row. Circle the animal moving in a different direction.

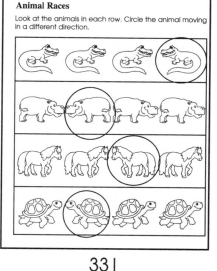

Be a Dinosaur Detective

Look at the picture below. Can you find **5** mistakes? Color them.

330

331

332

Opposites

Trace the words. Draw lines between the opposites.

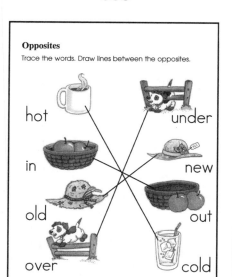

hot

in

old

over

under

new

out

cold

I Play Outside

In each box, circle the group of words that matches the words at the top of the box.

What Happens Next?

Look at the pictures. Write the sentences.

Will she go in the pool?

1. Will she go in the pool?

She will go in the pool.

2. She will go in the pool.

333

334

335

Humpty Dumpty

Write the words where they belong.

a   sat   had   the   fall   and   put   men

Humpty Dumpty ___sat___ on ___a___ wall.

Humpty Dumpty ___had___ a great ___fall___.

All ___the___ king's horses ___and___ all the

king's ___men___ couldn't ___put___

Humpty together again.

Over or Under

Look at the pictures. Tell whether the object is **over** or **under** the tree. Trace and color.

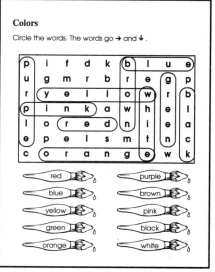

over   under

under   over

Colors

Circle the words. The words go → and ↓.

p	i	f	d	k	b	l	u	e
u	g	m	r	b	r	e	g	p
r	y	e	l	l	o	w	r	b
p	i	n	k	a	w	h	e	l
l	o	r	e	d	n	i	e	a
e	p	e	l	s	m	t	n	c
c	o	r	a	n	g	e	w	k

red   purple

blue   brown

yellow   pink

green   black

orange   white

336

337

338

Find the Rhyming Words

Look at each row. Circle the picture that rhymes with the first picture in the row.

339

Size Words

Trace and color.

big   small

short   tall

fast   slow

340

Who Needs This?

Look at the first picture in each row.
Color the picture that shows who needs it.

341

Small, Medium, Large

Look at the **small**, **medium**, and **large** doghouses.
Draw lines to match the dog to the doghouse.

342

Faces at the Zoo

Circle the animal that comes next in each row.

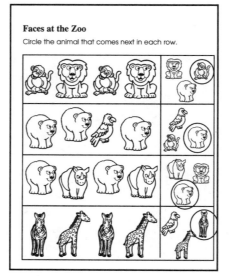

343

Pass the Ketchup

Color the triangles to lead the boy to the ketchup.

344

Square Surprises

Count the squares. Color them.

Circle to show how many squares you found.

1 2 3 4 5 6 7 8 9 (10)

345

Color by Number

Color the shapes below according to the color-by-number chart. You will see something that is fun to play with in the spring.

1 - yellow   2 - white   3 - blue   4 - green
5 - orange   6 - red   7 - black   8 - purple

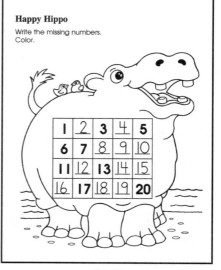

346

Happy Hippo

Write the missing numbers.
Color.

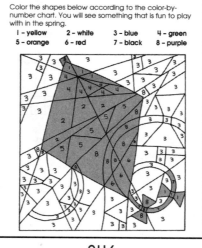

347

Lining Them Up

Unscramble and write the number words.

1. nnei   n i n e
2. neves   s e v e n
3. wetlev   t w e l v e
4. etreh   t h r e e
5. xis   s i x
6. etn   t e n
7. neo   o n e
8. efvi   f i v e
9. eeenlv   e l e v e n
10. wot   t w o
11. theig   e i g h t
12. rufo   f o u r

one
two
three
four
five
six
seven
eight
nine
ten
eleven
twelve

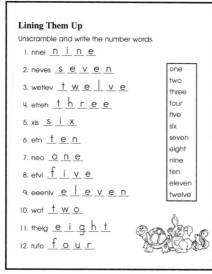

348

A Good Harvest

Connect the dots from **1** to **20**. Color.

349

Fall Hunt

Color the hidden pictures. Count each group and write the number in the correct box.

350

Barnyard Buddies

Find the hidden numbers **1** to **17**. Color them. Color the rest of the picture.

351

Nature Run

Color **5** flowers.   Color **7** suns.

Color **4** trees.   Color **6** birds.

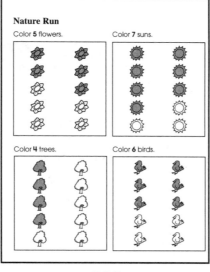

352

Count the Monkeys

Count the monkeys in each box. Write the number on the line.

353

Batter Up!

Find the baseballs ⚾. Color them red. Then color the rest of the picture. Can you find **13** baseballs in all?

354

Go Fish!

There are fifteen hidden fish in this picture. Draw a circle around each fish as you find it.

355

Sea Friends

Color the picture. Count the sea animals. Answer the question below.

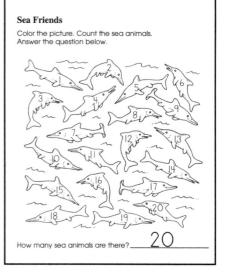

How many sea animals are there?   20

356

Daily Learning Drills Grade K

Hungry Baby Bunnies

Help Betsy Bunny find the carrots for her babies. Color the path that goes in order from **1** to **10**.

357

Skip Counting

Trace the numbers.

Count by twos.

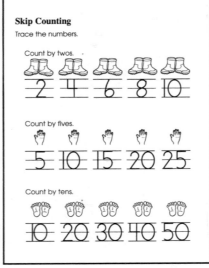

2 4 6 8 10

Count by fives.

5 10 15 20 25

Count by tens.

10 20 30 40 50

358

Monkeys Love Bananas!

Solve each problem. Write the answer on the line.

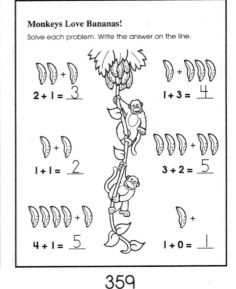

2 + 1 = 3

1 + 1 = 2

4 + 1 = 5

1 + 3 = 4

3 + 2 = 5

1 + 0 = 1

359

Away They Go

Cross out. Write how many are left.

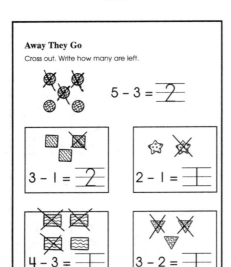

5 - 3 = 2

3 - 1 = 2

2 - 1 = 1

4 - 3 = 1

3 - 2 = 1

360

What's the Order?

first   second   third   fourth   fifth

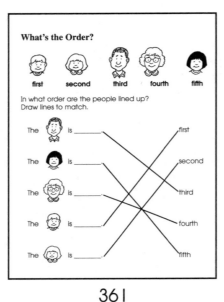

In what order are the people lined up?
Draw lines to match.

The ___ is ___   first

The ___ is ___   second

The ___ is ___   third

The ___ is ___   fourth

The ___ is ___   fifth

361

Do They Measure Up?

Use a ruler to measure the objects below.

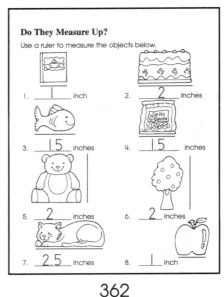

1. 1 inch
2. 2 inches
3. 1.5 inches
4. 1.5 inches
5. 2 inches
6. 2 inches
7. 2.5 inches
8. 1 inch

362

Body Count

Count your body parts. Cut out the body-part cards to match the number your body has. Glue under the correct numeral.

363

I Use My Senses

Draw pictures to show what you like to see, hear, smell, taste, and touch.

see	hear
Answers will vary.	
smell	taste
touch	

365

I Take Care of My Body

Does the picture show a way to take care of your body? Circle **yes** or **no**.

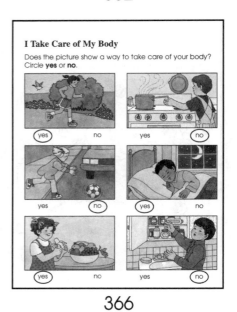

366

Delicious Food

Answers will vary.

Color the pictures. Say the words.
Check off the food you like to eat.

☐ apple   ☐ corn   ☐ egg

☐ beans   ☐ bread   ☐ cheese

☐ peach   ☐ orange   ☐ carrot

367

I Like Fruit!

Finish each sentence with the name of a fruit.

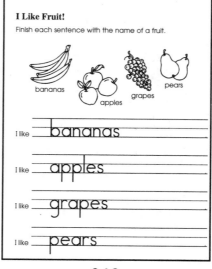

bananas   apples   grapes   pears

I like ___bananas___

I like ___apples___

I like ___grapes___

I like ___pears___

368

My Favorite Kind of Plant

Color the picture. then complete the sentences.

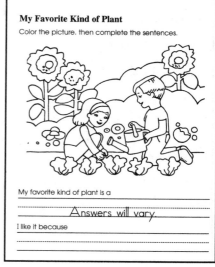

My favorite kind of plant is a

___Answers will vary.___

I like it because

371

Living or Not?

Color the pictures of living things.

pony	pig	ball
doll	lamb	snowman
rain	chicken	duck

372

At the Beach

Look at the picture. Find **3** living things.
Write their names.

umbrella
dolphin
palm tree
ball
sand bucket
child
chair

1. ___palm tree___

2. ___dolphin___

3. ___child___

373

Mother's Love

Draw a line from each baby animal to its mother.

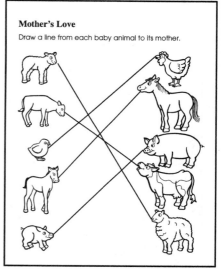

374

Shadow Match

Say the name of each animal and color. Draw
a line to match each animal with its shadow.

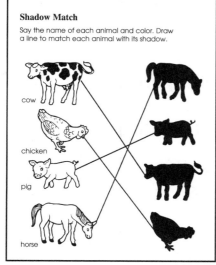

cow
chicken
pig
horse

375

Going to the Zoo

Circle the words. The words go → and ↓ .

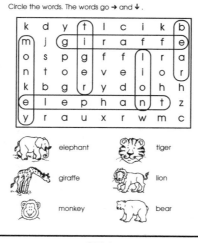

k	d	y	t	l	c	i	k	b
m	j	g	i	r	a	f	f	e
o	s	p	g	f	f	l	r	a
n	t	o	e	v	e	i	o	r
k	b	g	r	y	d	o	h	h
e	l	e	p	h	a	n	t	z
y	r	a	u	x	r	w	m	c

elephant   tiger

giraffe   lion

monkey   bear

376

In the Rain Forest

Circle the plants and animals that are in the picture.

377

Daily Learning Drills Grade K

Parts of a Crab

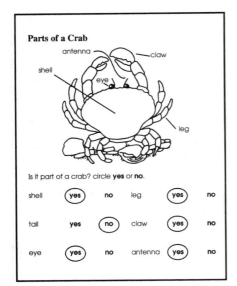

antenna
claw
shell
eye
leg

Is it part of a crab? circle **yes** or **no**.

shell	(yes)	no	leg	(yes)	no
tail	yes	(no)	claw	(yes)	no
eye	(yes)	no	antenna	(yes)	no

Going Home

Draw a line to help each animal find its home.

Animals, Animals Everywhere

Color the animals. Cut out the pictures. Paste them where they belong.

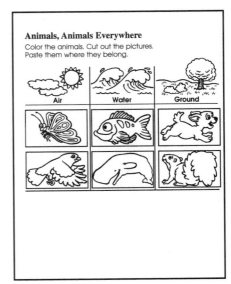

Air Water Ground

378
379
380

Dino Pet!

If you could have a pet dinosaur, what would it look like? Draw your dinosaur below. Write its name on the line.

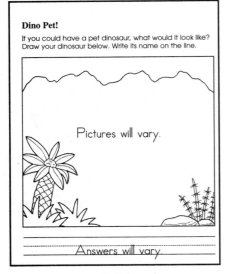

Pictures will vary.

Answers will vary.

Looking at the Seasons

Cross out the things that do not belong with each season.

spring fall

summer winter

I Am Special

Draw a picture of yourself. Write your name.

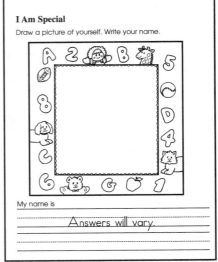

My name is

Answers will vary.

381
382
383

I Can Use These Things

Answers will vary.

Color the objects you can use.

Things I Like

Answers will vary.

Look at each picture. Say the word. Is it something you like? Check **yes** or **no**.

gift milk

yes ☐ no ☐   yes ☐ no ☐

dog books

yes ☐ no ☐   yes ☐ no ☐

384
385

My Favorite Things

Color the pictures of things you like.

Answers will vary.

386

Feelings

Trace. Draw the child's face to match the feeling.

happy   sad

Faces will vary.

proud   angry

389

I Am Happy

Color the pictures that make you feel happy.

Answers will vary.

390

My Fantastic Family

How many people are in your family? _____

Write their names.

_____

Answers will vary.

_____

_____

Draw a picture of your family.

391

Family Fun

Draw a picture of a family having fun inside the house.
Draw a picture of a family having fun outside.

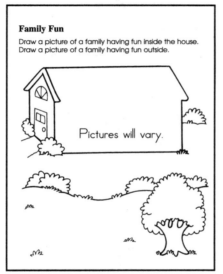

Pictures will vary.

392

Time for Chores   Answers will vary.

Read the rhyme. Then look at the pictures.
Circle the chores you help out with.

Jack and Jill went up the hill
To fetch a pail of water.
Jack fell down, and broke his crown,
And Jill came tumbling after.

wash dishes   wash the car   take out trash

set the table   iron clothes   make the bed

cook meals   put away toys   cut the grass

393

Toys   Answers will vary.

Color the pictures. Say the names of the toys.
Circle the toys you like to play with.

truck   blocks   ball

drum   doll   bat

pail   top   balloon

394

Who Helps You?

Circle the words. The words go → and ↓.

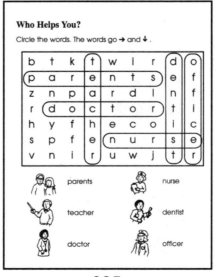

b	t	k	t	w	i	r	d	o
p	a	r	e	n	t	s	e	f
z	n	p	a	r	d	l	n	f
r	d	o	c	t	o	r	t	i
h	y	f	h	e	c	o	i	c
s	p	f	e	n	u	r	s	e
v	n	i	r	u	w	j	t	r

parents   nurse

teacher   dentist

doctor   officer

395

A Milking Maze

Can you help the farmers get to their cows? Read each clu[e]
Draw a path that goes by the dairy food named to the cow
Use a new color for each path.

I like to eat ice cream. I will milk Spotty.
I like to eat cheese. I will milk Dotty.
I like to eat yogurt. I will milk Lumpy.
I like to eat butter. I will milk Bumpy.

Dotty   Bumpy   Spotty   Lumpy

396

Places to Go

Look at each picture clue. Look in the Word Box for the place you would find that thing.
Write the word in the puzzle.

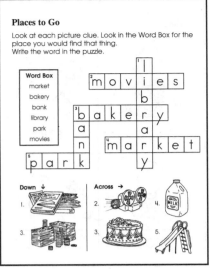

Word Box
market
bakery
bank
library
park
movies

Down ↓
Across →

397

What a Great Place!

Fill in the puzzle with words that name the pictures below.
Use the Word Box to help you.

1. e r a s e r
2. t e a c h e r
3. c h a l k
4. c r a y o n s
5. b o o k
6. p e n c i l

Word Box
teacher
pencil
book
crayons
eraser
chalk

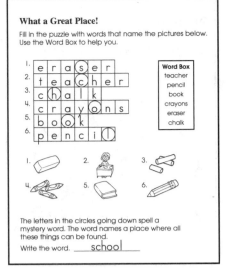

1.   2.   3.
4.   5.   6.

The letters in the circles going down spell a mystery word. The word names a place where all these things can be found.
Write the word. ___school___

398

Teacher's Helper

Lead the teacher to her chalkboard.

2 + 2 = 4

399

School Supplies

Color the pictures. Write the word for each picture.

pencil   glue   scissors   crayon

g l u e   c r a y o n

s c i s s o r s   p e n c i l

400

Reading Signs

Read each sign. Draw a line to the matching picture.

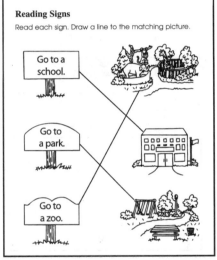

Go to a school.

Go to a park.

Go to a zoo.

401

Ways to Travel

Write a word for each picture.

boat   plane   car   train

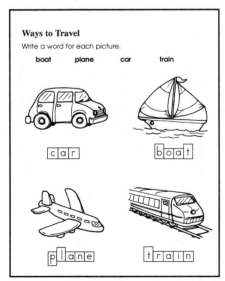

c a r   b o a t

p l a n e   t r a i n

402

Go For a Car Ride!

Choose the correct word below to complete each sentence. Write each word in the correct puzzle square.
Then read the black boxes from top to bottom to find another travel word!

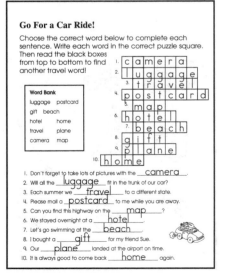

1. c a m e r a
2. l u g g a g e
3. t r a v e l
4. p o s t c a r d
5. m a p
6. h o t e l
7. b e a c h
8. g i f t
9. p l a n e
10. h o m e

Word Bank
luggage   postcard
gift   beach
hotel   home
travel   plane
camera   map

1. Don't forget to take lots of pictures with the ___camera___
2. Will all the ___luggage___ fit in the trunk of our car?
3. Each summer we ___travel___ to a different state.
4. Please mail a ___postcard___ to me while you are away.
5. Can you find this highway on the ___map___?
6. We stayed overnight at a ___hotel___
7. Let's go swimming at the ___beach___
8. I bought a ___gift___ for my friend Sue.
9. Our ___plane___ landed at the airport on time.
10. It is always good to come back ___home___ again.

403
